D. H. Lawrence

A red flower falls to its dim reflection

— Hush then, never a word.

一朵红花落向它朦胧的倒影

——嘘，别再发出一丝声音。

[英] 劳伦斯 著

吴笛 译

劳伦斯
诗选

英诗经典
名家名译

——
Selected Poems of
D. H. Lawrence
——

英　汉
对　　照

外语教学与研究出版社
FOREIGN LANGUAGE TEACHING AND RESEARCH PRESS
北京 BEIJING

意切情深信达雅

——序《英诗经典名家名译》

上小学前，爷爷就教导我要爱劳动，爱念诗。"劳动"是让我拾粪、浇菜、割驴草……"诗"是学念他一生中读过的唯一"诗集"《三字经》中的"人之初，性本善"等。我还算听话，常下地帮着干零活，偶尔也念诗。上中学后喜出望外地得知，最早的诗歌便是俺乡下人干重活时有意无意发出的"哎哟、哎哟"之类的号子声。老师说，这是鲁迅先生发现的。后来糊里糊涂考进北大，便懵懵懂懂向冯至、李赋宁、闻家驷等老师学习一些欧洲国家的诗歌。

大约十二天前，我正准备出访东欧和中亚时，北大、北外、党校三重校友兼教育部副部长郝平指示我为外语教学与研究出版社即将付印的《英诗经典名家名译》写篇序言。基于上述背景，我竟不自量力，欣欣然应允，飞机起飞不久就边拜读边写体会了。

一看目录，我在万米高空立即激动不已。译者全是令我肃然起敬又感到亲切的名字。

冰心是我初中时代的"作家奶奶"，我工作后曾专门找借口去拜访她在福建的故居。袁可嘉半个世纪前应邀从南大到北大讲英国文学史，我是自己搬着凳子硬挤进去旁听的幸运学生之一。王佐良先生是我读研究生时教授英国诗歌的。同学们爱听他的课，他大段引用原文从不看讲稿，我们常觉得他的汉语译文会比原文更精彩……穆旦、屠岸、江枫、杨德豫等我未曾有幸当面请教，从他们的作品中却受益良多，感激恨晚。

前辈翻译家们追求"信、达、雅"。落实这"三字经"却并非易事。

第一，在丰富多彩、良莠不齐的英文诗林中，译者要有足够高的先进理念和真知灼见去发现和选择思想水平高的作品。国产千里马尚需伯乐去认同，意识形态领域里的诗就更需要了。看诗的高下、文野，境界和情感永远是最重要的因素。我国《诗经》历久不衰，首先因为里面有"硕鼠，硕鼠，无食我黍！"这样政治上合民心的诗句，有"关关雎鸠，在河之洲……"这样传递真情的佳句。这套诗集选了许多跨世纪思想性极强的好诗。如雪莱《普罗米修斯的解放》中的警句："国王、教士与政客们摧毁了人类之花，当它还只是柔嫩的蓓蕾……"今天读起来仍发人深省。如莎士比亚在其第 107 号十四行诗中将和平与橄榄树的葱郁有机相连，上承两千多年前中国先哲"和为贵"的真谛，下接联合国大会此时此刻的紧急议题。这样的诗自然有人爱，有人信。

第二，诗源于生活。诗作者和译者都最好与百姓血肉相连。马克思曾与诗友调侃：诗人也得吃饭，别奢望写诗写饿了上帝会把盛着面包的篮子从天堂递下来。这套诗选中有许多生活气息浓醇、情意真切的诗。如出身佃农的彭斯在 18 世纪法国大革命后写的政治讽刺诗："我赞美主的威力无边！主将千万人丢在黑暗的深渊……""……阔人们日子过得真舒泰，穷人们活得比鬼还要坏！""……有的书从头到尾都是谎言，有的大谎还没有见于笔端。"写实和预言都相当准确。

第三，译文要忠实于原作，自身又要通畅、简洁、优美。这套诗集中，英文原作都是名符其实的经典。读诗最好读原文，但世界上大约有三千种语言，一个人会用来读诗的语言肯定少得可怜。为开阔视野、加强交流、增进友谊，读外国诗大多还得靠翻译。这套诗选中的译者都治学严谨，都酷爱祖国和外国优秀文化，译文是他们辛勤劳动的杰出成果。他们把拜伦的奔放、纪伯伦的靓丽、济慈的端庄、布莱克的纯真、华兹华斯的素净、叶芝的淡定、狄金森和弗罗斯特的质朴译得惟妙惟肖。读这样的译作，哲学上可受启迪，美学上可得滋润。这有益于读者的身心健康，能满足青年学生的好奇心和求知欲，也能为有关专家的进一步研讨提供方便。

不妨说，这套诗集中外皆宜，老少咸宜，会书中两种语文或其中一种的人皆宜。

李肇星

2011 年 9 月 14 日至 25 日自乌兰巴托（意为"红色勇士"）上空经莫斯科、明斯克（"交易地"）、塔什干（"石头城"）飞阿拉木图（"苹果城"）途中。

目 录

译序

　　他如同哈代，既以丰富的小说创作赢得了巨大的声誉，又以千首诗作奠定了他作为20世纪重要诗人的地位；他不同于哈代，后者是因晚年《无名的裘德》的出版受到了社会舆论的攻击和压力而放弃小说创作，潜心写诗，在近60岁时才出版第一本诗集，而前者在一生中却同时进行诗和小说创作，并在二十几岁就出版了第一本诗集。这位比哈代迟45年诞生（1885），而在哈代死后两年就追随他奔赴黄泉的文学巨匠，就是D. H. 劳伦斯。

　　然而，这位劳伦斯似乎还不如哈代幸运。哈代的诗歌成就历来受到庞德、奥登等著名诗人的赞赏，50年代后更是被一批青年诗人尊为楷模，被著名诗人菲利普·拉金推崇为"20世纪最伟大的诗人"；而劳伦斯则命途多舛，60年代之前，由于他的小说遭受查禁，他本来很有活力的诗歌也似乎受到株连，没有得到应有的重视，无怪乎有人曾经叹息道："假若劳伦斯只写诗歌，他一定会被看成是最重要的英语诗人之一。"[1] 劳伦斯本人在生前似乎也看出了这一点，他曾经不无悲观地说，他的作品要到三百年后才会

---

[1] David Perkins, *A History of Modern Poetry: From the 1890s to the High Modernist Mode*, Cambridge, MA: Harvard University Press, 1979, p. 439.

被人理解。[1] 然而，三百年时间实为长久，我们恐怕难以待到那时才对他评说是非。值得劳伦斯宽慰的是，如今，他作为 20 世纪重要的诗人和小说家，已经开始在世界上得到广泛承认，其作品已经开始被人理解和喜爱。

劳伦斯的诗歌是他一生中文学创作的重要组成部分，也是他一生中的欢乐、痛苦以及思想感受的重要记录。他的早期诗歌具有浓厚的自传色彩，如他自己所说，这些诗篇凑在一起，构成了一部充满激情的内心生活传记。这种自传色彩是他早期诗作的一大特点，在《爱情诗及其他》等早期诗集中，主题主要是爱情，尤其是诗集《瞧！我们走过来了！》更是一部心灵活动的诗的记录，是他与弗丽达结合的新婚曲，是爱的贺颂，是他们早期婚姻生活中欢乐与痛苦的记录。跟弗丽达结合在一起的第一年年底，劳伦斯曾写信给柯布金太太说："我常是爱情的祭司。"[2] 这句话正好概括了他早期诗歌的主题。

劳伦斯的早期诗歌，首先具有一种内在的诚实和明快的气质，他在诗中表现了画家的眼力，也表明了诗人的眼力，使诗的形象清新自然，生动逼真，具有动人的美感。同时，他的联想大胆而新鲜，比喻深刻而真切，不仅有着画家的视觉感受，还有着敏锐的触觉感受，他用具有触觉的语汇来塑造抒情诗形象，触击和打动读者的心灵。

其次，在劳伦斯的早期诗中，爱情与憎恨、兴奋与恐惧、美与冷酷等相对立的因素常常联结成一体，充满了矛盾，充满了神秘，如《致米莉娅姆的最后的话语》《金鱼草》等。在诗集《瞧！我们走过来了！》中，按作者自己的话说，"爱与恨的矛盾"也是"延续不断……"的。劳伦斯试图在这组诗中表现一对新婚夫妇心理上的关系，表现欢乐与痛苦以及爱与恨的冲突，无怪乎埃米·洛厄尔说，这组诗"构成了一部伟大的长篇小说，其容量甚至比《儿

1　Keith M. Sagar, *The Art of D. H. Lawrence*, Cambridge: Cambridge University Press, 1966, p. 1.

2　赫利·摩尔著：《劳伦斯传》（杨耐冬译），台湾志文出版社 1984 年版，第 167 页。

子与情人》还要大得多。"[1] 戏剧性的独白诗《农场之恋》集中体现了这一特色：当情人来临，燕子恐惧地逃出温暖的巢窝；鹧藏起优雅的脸，死寂般地躺下；兔子万分惊恐地拼命逃窜，但仍旧被这位情人所捕捉，他扔下被他杀死的兔子，便去拥抱等待他的女人，手臂像举起的利剑抵住她的胸膛，仍旧散发兔皮血腥味的手指在女人身上抚摩不停……这个女人感觉到一股甜蜜的火浪流经全身，觉得自己在火浪中慢慢死去，并且认为死亡是件美好的事情。

再则，劳伦斯在早期诗中擅长运用象征和比喻等手法来表现自己的观点。他常将素材重点加以暗示，并非直言。如在上述的《农场之恋》中，他并没有告诉我们性爱与死亡在本质上是相互接近的，但他通过一系列的意象、较为笨拙的韵律和显得粗糙的情节剧的独白等手法，来使我们感觉到这种相似性。再如，在《瞧！我们走过来了！》中，劳伦斯对早期生活的欢乐与痛苦也不是直接倾诉，而多半是通过诗人和弗丽达的感受来反射的。他使用的比喻颇具匠心，如在上述《农场之恋》中，他以傍晚的红霞来比喻爱情的伤痕，把张开的手臂比作举起的利剑，把双眼比作两块黑铁，把情欲比作甜蜜的火浪等，这些比喻都恰到好处地服务了诗的主题，深化了诗的形象。

如果说劳伦斯的早期诗歌主要是自传性的记述，那么，他到了创作中期，已摆脱了这种自传的束缚，而在非人类的自然界开拓了新的诗歌天地。他1923年出版的《鸟·兽·花》被认为"是对诗歌艺术的独特贡献"[2]。他通过动植物世界，以现代风格表现了现代人的感受，所以《现代诗歌史》的编著者把《鸟·兽·花》与T. S. 艾略特的《荒原》等诗作，共同列为现代派文学的划时代的作品。《鸟·兽·花》这部诗集，劳伦斯是于1920年开始动笔，完成于1923年，多半写于意大利的西西里岛。这些诗描述和反映各

1　David Perkins, *A History of Modern Poetry: From the 1890s to the High Modernist Mode*, p. 439.

2　《简明不列颠百科全书（第5卷）》，中国大百科全书出版社1986年版，第136页。

种各样的水果、树木、花朵、野兽、家禽、鸟雀等非人类的动植物的生活。这些动植物是隐喻和象征，劳伦斯通过它们来表达自己的心思、观念、情感。作为叙述者和评论者，劳伦斯经常在诗中出现，因此，读着这些诗，有一种类似谈心时的愉悦；这些诗生气勃勃，清晰敏锐，措辞巧妙，富有个性。尽管这些动植物是作为隐喻和象征来使用的，但作者对它们作了生动逼真的细节描写，也作了富有力度的深层次的挖掘，使人们感到植物有情，动物有智。他往往凭借一个小小的动植物，来使自己的想象自由驰骋，使自己的才艺得到充分的发挥，从而曲折地反映生活，反映他对世道人心的忧虑。这是对华兹华斯、哈代传统的继承和突破，也正是这一点，对尔后的特德·休斯等诗人产生了巨大的影响。同时，这些诗也常常通过表层的信息来反映深刻的、多角度和多层次的含义，如《无花果》《乌龟的呼喊》等。后者通过乌龟的一声叫喊来反映原始本能和强大的生命力，把性看成是被血液所领悟的隐藏的神秘力量，所以有的人称该诗是劳伦斯诗中最有力量、最具生气的一首。这种多层次的含义也较为突出地反映在著名的《蛇》中，该诗表达了一种矛盾心理的特别情结。诗中有一种"我所受的教育"的声音要杀死"从大地的躯体中冒出来的燃烧的大肠"，又有另一种声音对蛇类寄予深切的同情。诗中，这条蛇被想象性地转化为一个象征，一种神秘力量，于是，混合起来的担忧、欢欣、迷惑、惊恐、崇敬不仅引向了蛇类，而且也引向了交织在诗中的黑暗、死亡、下界、爱情、神性的联系和内涵。

《鸟·兽·花》中，不仅有对下界黑暗的歌颂，也有对现世、对生命的向往，《杏花》一诗可以说是一曲优美的生命的颂歌，杏花是复活的象征。诗人把寒冬腊月的黝黑的杏树枝比作"生锈的钢铁"，然而，待到初春，这钢铁却能绽开、萌芽，喷放出束束鲜花。在诗中，诗人不是把意象作为实例或装饰来使用，而是以意象来进行思维，用艾略特的话来说，是"思想知觉化"。

自 1923 年 2 月完成《鸟·兽·花》之后，将近六年时间，劳伦斯没有写过任何诗作;直到生命的晚期,他才又开始提笔作诗。1928 年 12 月 10 日,他写道:"我正在从事创作一些小小的三色紫罗兰——一种诗歌。而实际上是思想,全都是片断,相当有趣。"[1] 第一卷《三色紫罗兰》出版于 1929 年,后来,在劳伦斯死后,意象派大师理查德·奥尔丁顿又编辑出版了《三色紫罗兰续编》。三色紫罗兰一词"pansies",在法语中拼为 pensées,具有"三色紫罗兰"和"思想"两种词义,因此,该诗集及其续编可以看作是用诗写成的随想录。这些诗有着独有的清新与直率,采用自由的韵律来自由地表达作者的人生观、宗教观、爱情观等。这时,他的思想已经成形,而使他思想成形的人物有达尔文、马克思、尼采、爱因斯坦以及弗洛伊德。他们的集体影响,就使得劳伦斯有了一种无所遁逃的压力感,也使得他诗中所表现的思想有着不可调和的矛盾:一方面他认为上帝不复存在,另一方面又认为上帝是自然界"强大无比的推动力";一方面他放弃宗教信仰,另一方面又常常认为生命本身就是一种宗教表现;一方面他认为爱情应该永恒不变,另一方面又认为爱情如同鲜花,不断地凋谢与绽放;一方面他歌颂疏离之感,歌颂孤独之美,另一方面又描述生活的和谐,描述与大自然的接触和沟通而产生的触觉感受;他嘲讽资产阶级,否定西方文明,但他并没有追随马克思主义;他既反对资本主义,又反对布尔什维克,他想打倒工资,打倒金钱,以神秘化的宗教信仰为基础,建立自己的空想社会主义。大概正是出于这一原因,奥尔丁顿才写道:"几乎所有的《三色紫罗兰》和《荨麻》都是出于劳伦斯的神经质,而不是出于他的自我。"这种说法不无道理,但未免言过其实,因为两部诗集中仍有许许多多卓越的诗篇。这些诗不仅透彻地表达了劳伦斯的思想,而且也表现了劳伦斯独有的艺术特色,因此,这些诗至今仍有着较高的认识价值。比如在《我们是生命的传送者》一诗中,作者认为人应当工

1　Keith M. Sagar, *The Art of D. H. Lawrence*, p. 1.

作，应当奉献，把自己的生命投入到工作之中。

在《三色紫罗兰》中，劳伦斯既有乐观的一面，他提倡"在闪光和燃烧中奉献自己，／快乐地扑闪着欢欣的生命；／身披光彩，／闪闪发光地走向外部世界"(《自我保护》)，但也有悲观的一面，他对中产阶级、对金钱与工业革命等都充满了失望与憎恨(《我嘛，是个爱国者》)，因此，他寻求解脱。爱情作为解脱最终归于失败，于是他找到了死亡，歌颂死亡的欢乐，认为经过无比痛苦的死亡体验，便会出现身后的欢乐，在死亡的巨大空间里，身后的轻风把我们亲吻成人性的花朵(《死亡的欢乐》)；他认为只有在死中才能复生。

而这种死亡意识则是他晚期著名诗集《最后的诗》(死后出版，1932) 的中心主题。如果说他早期是"爱情的祭司"，那么这时，他已从青年时代的"爱情的祭司"转变成了"死亡的歌手"。

该诗集是以《凤凰》一诗结尾的，这种自行焚死，然后由灰中复生的凤凰意象可以说是该诗集中具有代表性的意象。晚期，劳伦斯很受意大利伊特拉斯坎地方古宗教主义以及伊特拉斯坎地方艺术的影响。1927 年 4 月，他发现了伊特拉斯坎古墓群，而进入被发掘的古墓的生理行为，后来也被劳伦斯用来作为迈向下界、拥抱死亡的象征。在一个伊特拉斯坎王子的墓中，劳伦斯在许多殉葬品之中发现了一条铜制的小船，他曾在游记《伊特拉斯坎地方》中写道："这是一艘把王子送往另一世界的灵船。"于是，这艘铜制小灵船也成了他的著名诗作《灵船》里的中心意象。劳伦斯在诗中表述：秋天的苹果，掉落到地上，腐烂，释放出种子来获得新生。灵魂也是一样，人死之时，灵魂逃离躯体，因此，得制作灵船，装上逃离躯体的灵魂；告别旧的自我，通往湮灭之乡。灵船在黑暗的死亡之洋上没有目标地航行，直至完全消失，抵达湮灭。然而，"从永恒中"分离出一条细线，破除黑暗，迎来黎明，灵船归来了。因此，灵魂又找到了新的自我，像玫瑰一般萌发，开始新生，"用宁静填塞心房"。由此可见，灵船的意象仍等同于凤凰的意象，作者借助灵船的意象，表现生命不息，灵魂不灭，死中复生，周而复始这一思想。同时也应看到，他歌颂死亡，是为了赞扬新生，他唱起死亡之歌，是为了让生命之歌更有活力，这是他死亡观中较积极的一面。当然，劳伦斯的这种死亡观，这种对死亡的超越感，是不太令人信服的。他在临死前一直从事着《灵船》的创作，或许是他感到了死亡的威胁，因而对复生产生了强烈的向往？因为他在《艰难的死亡》一诗中表现了这种微弱的希望："也许经过痛苦的湮灭历程／生命仍是我们的组成部分。"

　　然而，死神是无情的，它于 1930 年夺去了劳伦斯的生命，而且也不可能让他像凤凰那样从灰烬中重生。可是，值得九泉之下的劳伦斯庆幸的是，从某种意义上说，他以自己的艺术作品为自己制作了一条"灵船"，就像普希金用诗歌为自己建造了一座非人工的纪念碑，他那通向黑暗的湮灭之乡的灵魂又在他的作品中萌发出来，绽放并且永存在他不朽的艺术作品之中。他的诗歌受到了人们的理解和喜爱，1972 年《劳伦斯诗选》的编选者 K. M. 塞格尔在该书导言中引用柯尔律治评论浪漫派大师华兹华斯的话来赞美劳伦斯的诗："他的诗令人百读不厌，每次重读都有新鲜感。虽然读者能充分理解这些作品，但任何时代都很少有人能达到这些诗的思想深度，或有如此深入探讨的勇气。"我们认为，这番话是颇具概括性的。

劳伦斯

诗选

On the Road

I am out alone on the road;

From the low west windows the cold light flows

Along where my slow feet never trode;

I wish I knew where this pale road goes.

Soon the western windows of the sky

With shutters of clouded night will close.

And we'll still be together, the road and I

Together, wherever the dumb road goes.

The wind chases by me, and over the corn

Pale shadows flee from us as if from their foes

And save for me the road is forlorn

For none go whither this long road goes.

In the sky the low, tired moon goes out,

Wearily, through the oaks, the night wind blows,

Pale, sleepy flowers are tossed about

As the wind asks whither the dark road goes.

Away on the hillside wakes a star,

Below, the pit-lights glitter in rows

在路上

我独自一人走上道路；
寒冷的光芒流出西面的窗户，
流向我双足从未踏过的地方；
但愿我知道这苍白的道路通往何方。

遮上了阴暗夜幕的西面天窗
很快就会完全关闭。
可我与道路不会分离，
不管这沉默的道路通向哪里。

轻风在我身边追逐，在麦田之上，
苍白的阴影逃离我们如同躲避灾难，
别人觉得这道路极为凄凉，
没人会光顾这条长路通往的地方。

在空中，低垂、疲倦的月亮走了出来，
夜晚的风透过橡树困乏地吹拂，
昏昏欲睡的苍白花朵摇曳不定，
当风儿询问黑暗的道路通往何处。

那边山坡上一颗星星苏醒过来，
下方，一排排的矿灯闪闪发光，

That is my home where the lamp gleams afar

But it's the other way that my dark road now goes.

I am tired of this journey, it is stupid and chill

The road winds forever, and which of us knows

What lies over the next dark hill?

Anywhere, nowhere, the dead road goes.

When morning comes, I find me a love

And I'll lie in her lap where the world's wild rose

Blushes and flaunts in the sunshine above.

Why should I care where the old road goes?

那是我的家，灯光在远处闪烁，
但现在这黑暗的道路通往相反的方向。

我厌倦了这愚笨、扫兴的旅程，
道路永远蜿蜒向前，谁能查明
下一个黑暗的山丘后有些什么？
这条死亡的道路毫无目标地延伸。

当清晨来临，我为自己寻来恋人，
我会躺进她的怀抱，那个世界的
野蔷薇在阳光中显现出绯红。
我干吗挂虑这条古老道路的去向？

Love Comes Late

I did not know Love had settled down on me:
He came like a sea-gull, sinking with uplifted wings down
    on a slow-breathing sea,
And hardly disturbing wavering shimmer
Of sunset, but merging unnoticed into the rosy glimmer.

It settled so softly I was all unaware,
And the flush faded and it came dark; I slept, still ignorant
    love was there,
Till a dream came trembling through my flesh in the night
And I woke, wondering who touched me with such fear
    and delight.

With the first dawn I rose to look in the glass
And I started with pleasure, for in the night it had come to pass
That the time-threads spun across my face
Had been woven into a glorious mesh, like a bridal lace.

I have a charm like laughter through a veil,
Like a girl's tinkling merriment at night when the sea is pale;
My heart has a warmth like this sea where the dawn
Has strewn myriad twinkling poppy-petals down the path
    of a love late born.

迟来的爱情

我不知道爱情已居于我的身上：
他像海鸥一样来临，扬起双翼掠过缓缓呼吸的大海，
几乎没有惊动摇曳的落日余晖，
但不知不觉已融进玫瑰的色彩。

它轻柔地降临，我丝毫没有觉察，
红光消隐，它深入黑暗；我沉睡，浑然不知爱情来到
　　这里，
直到一个梦在夜间颤悠悠地经过我的肉体，
于是我醒来，不知道是谁以如此的恐惧和喜悦将我
　　触击。

随着第一道曙光，我起身照镜，
我愉快地开始，因为在夜间
我脸上所纺起的时光之线
已经织成美丽的面纱，如同新娘的花边。

我拥有的魅力，如同一阵笑声透过面纱，
像姑娘在大海苍白的夜间有着叮当作响的欢畅；
我心中的温暖，如同海洋；沿着迟来的爱情之路，
曙光撒下无数片片闪耀的罂粟花瓣。

All these glittering sea-birds wheel and fret

Below me, complaining that never, never yet

Has the warmth of a night kiss spread through their blood

Sending them rioting at dawn down the lane of scarlet poppy

    petals strewn across the flood.

所有这些闪闪发光的海鸟烦躁地飞旋

在我的下方，抱怨夜间亲吻的温暖

从未渗进它们的血液，促使它们

在清晨恣情地追逐撒入水中的红色罂粟花瓣。

A Decision

She is sweet and soft-throated,
Her eyes glow, as she
Tunes her voice, many noted
For me.

Her warm red lips
Are budded, as she
With a quick kiss clips
Them to me.

Her hair's live curl
Clutches for me.
Alas! Tossed back in my hearts swirl
Is she.

判定

她甜蜜逗人，嗓音柔和，
当她为我调整
抑扬顿挫的歌喉，
喜色燃烧在她的眼睛。

她温暖的朱唇
像含苞待放的鲜花，
当她把一记疾速的亲吻
印上我的面颊。

她活泼的缕缕鬓发
为我形成一道道波纹，
哎呀！是她在我心中
激起旋涡翻滚。

Separated

Ah I know how you have sought me,
The books that you have touched cleave close to me,
The withering flowers that days ago you brought me
Speak in half-bitter scent your dream of me.

And ever, ere I come, you have departed,
And it must be so ever, we must not meet,
And ever I see your traces, broken-hearted
Hear re-echo your slow, reluctant feet.

分离

我知道你怎样将我寻觅，
你触过的书籍偎在我的身边，
你前几日带给我的正在枯萎的花朵
用苦涩的芬芳诉说你梦中的醋甜。

我还没有到达，你就辞别而去，
必将永远分离，没有相见时分，
可我一旦看见你留下的形迹，
破碎的心就重新回荡你悠悠的足音。

Erotic

And when I see the heavy red fleece
Of the creeper on the breast of the house opposite
Lift and ruffle in the wind,
I feel as if feathers were lifted and shook
On the breast of a robin that is fluttered with pain,
And my own breast opens in quick response
Arid its beat of pain is distributed on the wind.

And when I see the trees sway close,
Lean together and lift wild arms to embrace,
I lift my breast and lean forward.
Holding down my leaping arms.

And when black leaves stream out in a trail down the wind,
I raise my face so it shall wreathe me
Like a tress of black hair,
And I open my lips to take a strand of keen hair.

And when I see the thick white body of train-smoke break
And fly fast away,
I stifle a cry of despair.

情诗

当我看到对面房屋的窗腰上
爬藤那沉重的红色叶簇
在风中昂扬飘拂，
我感到似乎在痛苦振翼的知更鸟
胸脯上竖起并且晃动着羽毛，
我自己的胸膛也回应般地迅速敞开，
它痛苦的敲击声散在风中。

当我看到树木亲密地俯身，
偎在一起，伸开野性的手臂接受拥抱，
我就昂起胸脯向前偎依，
并且垂下我的挥起的双臂。

当黑色的树叶顺着劲风纷纷飘扬，
我昂起胸膛，好让它在我脸上织起花环，
像一束黑色的长发在我脸上轻触，
我启开双唇接受美丽的发束。

当我看见浓烟的白色躯体
破碎并且急速消逝，
我闷死一声绝望的叫喊。

A Kiss

A red flower falls to its dim reflection
  —Hush then, never a word.
A red flower falls to its red reflection,
The shadow dances up in affection,
And two are one in sweet connection,
  —Never a sound was heard.

Something has gone down the silent river
  —What does the robin say?
Silver slow goes by the river,
Far off in gold the willows quiver,
And further still 'neath the sunset gather
  Red flowers that have floated away.

亲吻

一朵红花落向它朦胧的倒影
　　——嘘，别再发出一丝声音。
一朵红花落向它红色的倒影，
倒影向上浮动，充满深情，
两者融合成为甜蜜的整体，
　　——再也听不见一丝声音。

寂静的河面上有东西飘过
　　——知更鸟在评说什么？
银白缓慢地从河边飘过
远方，柳树在金光中战栗，
更远的地方，在暮色的下面，
　　漂走的红花在悄然聚集。

Cherry Robbers

Under the long dark boughs, like jewels red
    In the hair of an Eastern girl
Hang strings of crimson cherries, as if had bled
    Blood-drops beneath each curl.

Under the glistening cherries, with folded wings
    Three dead birds lie:
Pale-breasted throstles and a blackbird, robberlings
    Stained with red dye.

Against the haystack a girl stands laughing at me,
    Cherries hung round her ears.
Offers me her scarlet fruit: I will see
    If she has any tears.

樱桃偷盗者

像东方姑娘发间的红色珠宝，
　　在黑沉沉的长枝下面
挂着一串串鲜红的樱桃，
　　仿佛滴滴鲜血渗出了发卷。

在熠熠闪光的樱桃的下面，
　　躺着三只死鸟，翅膀合拢：
两只白胸脯的画眉和一只乌鸦，
　　盗贼们的身上沾染了鲜红。

干草堆旁站着一位姑娘对我微笑，
　　颗颗樱桃悬挂在她耳朵周围。
她向我奉献红色的果实，我将观望
　　她的眼中是否会流出几滴泪水。

Love on the Farm

What large, dark hands are those at the window
Grasping in the golden light
Which weaves its way through the evening wind
    At my heart's delight?

Ah, only the leaves! But in the west
I see a redness suddenly come
Into the evening's anxious breast—
    'Tis the wound of love goes home!

The woodbine creeps abroad
Calling low to her lover:
    The sun-lit flirt who all the day
    Has poised above her lips in play
    And stolen kisses, shallow and gay
    Of pollen, now has gone away—
She woos the moth with her sweet, low word:
And when above her his moth-wings hover
Then her bright breast she will uncover
And yield her honey-drop to her lover.

Into the yellow, evening glow
Saunters a man from the farm below;

农场之恋

是谁黝黑的大手扒着窗框
在金色的光芒之中,
这金光在夜风中扑闪扑闪
　　使我心口快乐无穷?

啊, 只是树叶! 但是在西方
我看见一朵鲜红突然来临
进入夜晚的焦急的乳房——
　　这是爱情的伤痕返回家庭!

五叶地锦爬到外面
对她的情人轻声呼唤:
　　沐浴阳光求爱者
　　整天悬在她唇上嬉戏
　　偷盗了花粉轻柔愉快的亲吻,
　　现在他已经消逝——
她低声甜蜜地向飞蛾求爱,
当他在她的上方扑翼盘旋,
她将敞露美好欢快的乳房
把蜜一般的乳汁向情人奉献。

一个男人从下方的农场
信步逛进黄色的暮光;

Leans, and looks in at the low-built shed
Where the swallow has hung her marriage bed.

    The bird lies warm against the wall.

    She glances quick her startled eyes

    Towards him, then she turns away

    Her small head, making warm display

    Of red upon the throat. Her terrors sway

    Her out of the nest's warm, busy ball,

    Whose plaintive cry is heard as she flies

    In one blue stoop from out the sties

    Into the twilight's empty hall.

Oh, water-hen, beside the rushes
Hide your quaintly scarlet blushes,
Still your quick tail, lie still as dead,
Till the distance folds over his ominous tread!

The rabbit presses back her ears,
Turns back her liquid, anguished eyes
And crouches low; then with wild spring
Spurts from the terror of his oncoming;
To be choked back, the wire ring
Her frantic effort throttling:

    Piteous brown ball of quivering fears!
Ah, soon in his large, hard hands she dies.

俯身探视低矮的小屋，
那里面燕子已垒起了婚床。

　　鸟儿温暖地靠墙而躺。
　　她向他快速投过惊奇的目光，
　　然后掉转小小的脑袋，
　　将喉上的鲜红热情地展现。
　　她的恐惧把她从温暖的巢中摇出，
　　像忙碌的球，她的哀鸣清晰可辨，
　　当她以一个蓝色的俯冲，从陋屋
　　冲进空荡荡的晚霞的庭院。

啊，鹬啊，在灯芯草旁边
藏起你优雅的怕羞的脸，
静下你敏捷的尾，死寂般地躺下，
直至那远方笼罩住他不祥的步伐！

兔子缩回耳朵，转回
清澄、烦恼的眼睛，蜷起身子；
然后以疯狂的跳跃
猛然冲出他行将逼近的恐惧；
可是铁环把她拖住，
扼杀了她疯狂的努力：
　　不寒而栗的凄惨球体！
啊，她很快死在他巨大残忍的手中。

And swings all loose from the swing of his walk!
Yet calm and kindly are his eyes
And ready to open in brown surprise
Should I not answer to his talk
Or should he my tears surmise.

I hear his hand on the latch, and rise from my chair
Watching the door open; he flashes bare
His strong teeth in a smile, and flashes his eyes
In a smile like triumph upon me; then careless-wise
He flings the rabbit soft on the table board
And comes towards me: ah! the uplifted sword
Of his hand against my bosom! and oh, the broad
Blade of his glance that asks me to applaud
His coming! With his hand he turns my face to him
And caresses me with his fingers that still smell grim
Of the rabbit's fur! God, I am caught in a snare!
I know not what fine wire is round my throat;
I only know I let him finger there
My pulse of life, and let him nose like a stoat
Who sniffs with joy before he drinks the blood.

从他走路的摇晃中摇得松散！
然而他的眼睛平静善良，
乐意在褐色的惊奇中睁圆，
假若我不回应他的交谈
或者他猜疑我的泪眼。

我听见他拉开门闩的声音，便从椅上起身
观看门被打开；他光秃秃地闪动
微笑中的强健的牙齿，以及笑容可掬的眼睛，
仿佛已把我战胜；随后轻率而精明地
把软绵绵的兔子抛掷在桌板之中，
并且朝我走来：啊！他的手如同举起的利剑
正好对准我的胸膛！
哦，他以那咄咄逼人的目光
要我欢呼他的来临！他伸手扳转我的脸，
用手指在我身上抚摩不停，
手指上仍旧残忍地散发兔皮气味，
天哪，我被抓进了陷阱！
我不知道什么样美好的绳索绕在我喉上；
我只知我让他用手指捻摸我的生命，
捻摸我的命脉，让他鼬一般地伸出鼻子，
在吸血之前津津有味地闻了又闻。

And down his mouth comes to my mouth! and down

His bright dark eyes come over me, like a hood

Upon my mind! his lips meet mine, and a flood

Of sweet fire sweeps across me, so I drown

Against him, die, and find death good.

他的嘴滑向我的嘴！他明亮的黑眼睛
来到我的脸前，像黑铁盖罩住我的心灵！
他的双唇撞上了我的双唇，
一股甜蜜的火浪掠过我的全身。
于是我沉溺于他的火浪之中，
慢慢死去，发现死亡是件美妙的事情。

Lightning

I felt the lurch and halt of her heart

    Next my breast, where my own heart was beating;

And I laughed to feel it plunge and bound,

And strange in my blood-swept ears was the sound

    Of the words I kept repeating,

Repeating with tightened arms, and the hot blood's blindfold art.

Her breath flew warm against my neck,

    Warm as a flame in the close night air;

And the sense of her clinging flesh was sweet

Where her arms and my neck's thick pulse could meet.

    Holding her thus, could I care

That the black night hid her from me, blotted out every speck?

I leaned in the darkness to find her lips

    And claim her utterly in a kiss,

When the lightning flew across her face

And I saw her for the flaring space

    Of a second, like snow that slips

From a roof, inert with death, weeping "Not this! Not this!"

A moment there, like snow in the dark

    Her face lay pale against my breast,

闪电

我感觉到在我胸口，在我心脏跳动之处，
　　她的心脏迈起了蹒跚的步履，
我欢笑地感觉到它上下跳动，
奇怪，在我清除了血液的耳朵里，
　　有我不断重复之词的声音，
重复着，双臂绷紧，以热血的看不见的技艺。

她的呼吸温暖地掠过我的颈项，
　　温暖得如同闷热之夜的一团火焰；
感觉到她紧贴的肉体是多么甜蜜，
当她的双臂与我颈部脉搏贴成一片。
　　如此紧搂，我难道担心
黑夜会把她藏走，抹除每一个印痕？

我在黑暗中俯身寻找她的樱唇
　　并把她完全索取在一记亲吻，
这时，一道闪电掠过她的脸蛋，
我看到了她，靠这瞬间闪烁的亮光，
　　像从屋顶上落下的雪
死一般苍白无力，哭着说："不要这样，不要这样！"

紧接着，像黑暗中的雪，
　　她惨白的脸紧偎在我的胸口，

Pale love lost in a thaw of fear

And melted in an icy tear,

And open lips, distressed;

A moment; then darkness shut the lid of the sacred ark.

And I heard the thunder, and felt the rain,

And my arms fell loose, and I was dumb.

Almost I hated her, sacrificed;

Hated myself, and the place, and the iced

Rain that burnt on my rage; saying: Come

Home, come home, the lightning has made it too plain!

苍白的爱情失却在融解的恐惧，
化入寒冷如冰的泪流，

　　融进悲痛的张开的嘴唇；
然后，黑暗关闭了神圣的方舟。

我听到了雷鸣，我感到了雨声，

　　我的双臂松弛下来，哑然失语。
我几乎憎恨她，这个牺牲品；
憎恨这块地方，憎恨我自己，

　　憎恨使我怒火中烧的冷雨；
回家吧，快回家，闪电使一切平淡无奇！

A Baby Running Barefoot

When the bare feet of the baby beat across the grass
The little white feet nod like white flowers in the wind,
They poise and run like puffs of wind that pass
Over water where the weeds are thinned.

And the sight of their white playing in the grass
Is winsome as a little robin's song, so fluttering;
Or like two butterflies that settle on a glass
Cup for a moment, soft little wing-beats uttering.

And I wish that the baby would tack across here to me
Like a wind-shadow running on a pond, so she could stand
With two little bare white feet upon my knee
And I could feel her feet in either hand

Cool as syringa buds in morning hours,
Or firm and silken as young peony flowers.

赤脚跑步的婴孩

那婴孩的白脚敲击着草坪，
小小的白脚像白花在风中摇晃，
停停跑跑如同一阵阵轻风
在水草稀疏的水面上游荡。

一双白脚在草中的游戏，
像知更鸟歌声一样迷人，飘忽不定；
或像暂且落在玻璃杯上的蝴蝶两只，
拍击羽翼，发出温柔之声。

我真的盼望婴孩朝我奔来，
就像风影在池水上奔跑，
一双白净的赤足伫于我的膝盖，
我能两手感觉到她的双脚

像清晨的山梅花苞凉爽清纯，
像新开的牡丹花结实、柔润。

Aware

Slowly the moon is rising out of the ruddy haze,

Divesting herself of her golden shift, and so

Emerging white and exquisite; and I in amaze

See in the sky before me, a woman I did not know

I loved, but there she goes, and her beauty hurts my heart;

I follow her down the night, begging her not to depart.

发觉

慢慢地，月亮从红润的云雾中升起，
脱去她金色的衬衣，于是浮现
一片皎洁，美丽无比；我怀着惊奇
发觉我无意中爱上的女人出现在蓝天，
她在那儿走动，她的妖娆刺痛我心怀，
整个夜间我紧随着她，恳求她不要离开。

A White Blossom

A tiny moon as small and white as a single jasmine flower
Leans all alone above my window, on night's wintry bower,
Liquid as lime tree blossom, soft as brilliant water or rain
She shines, the first white love of my youth, passionless
and in vain.

一朵白花

月儿娇小玲珑、白皙皎洁，像一朵孤单的茉莉花。
她孑然一身，悬挂在我窗口，偎倚在冬夜的家；
明亮清澈，似菩提之花；柔和晶莹，如清泉或细雨，
她，我青春的白色初恋，没有激情，枉然地把银辉抛洒。

A Winter's Tale

Yesterday the fields were only grey with scattered snow,
And now the longest grass-leaves hardly emerge;
Yet her deep footsteps mark the snow, and go
On towards the pines at the hills' white verge.

I cannot see her, since the mist's pale scarf
Obscures the dark wood and the dull orange sky;
But she's waiting, I know, impatient and cold, half
Sobs struggling into her frosty sigh.

Why does she come so promptly, when she must know
She's only the nearer to the inevitable farewell?
The hill is steep, on the snow my steps are slow—
Why does she come, when she knows what I have to tell?

冬天的故事

昨天，雪花飘零，田野一片灰蒙，
现在，最长的草叶儿也被白雪覆盖；
然而她在雪地印下一串深深的脚印，
一步步地通往雪山坡上的松柏。

我看不见她的倩影，宛如纱巾的浓雾
罩住了幽暗的树林和黯淡的橙色天空；
但我知道她在焦虑地等待，全身寒冷，
压低的悲哽不时冲进她冰霜般的叹息之中。

为什么她走得如此迅速，她应当知道，
与这注定的离别，她是唯一有关的人物？
雪山险峻，在雪地上我脚步缓慢——
她为何赴约，她应当知道我有话儿倾诉？

Return

Now I am come again, to you who have so desired
My coming, why do you look away from me?
Why burns your cheek against me? how have I inspired
Such anger as sets your mouth unwontedly?

Now here I sit while you break the music beneath
Your bow; for broken it is, and hurting to hear.
Cease then from music! Does anguish of absence bequeath
But barbed aloofness when I would draw near?

归来

我又回到你身边，既然你如此盼望
我的归来，可你为什么把脸扭向一边？
你的面颊为何在我跟前涨得绯红？
是什么惹得你生气，嘴儿噘得尖尖？

我坐了下来，你却拉起琴弓，击出乐声，
但击出的琴声是如此破碎，刺耳难听，
别再拉了！难道分离的痛苦只会使你
对渴望亲近的心灵赠送带刺的骄矜？

The Appeal

You, Helen, who see the stars
As mistletoe berries burning in a black tree,
You surely, seeing I am a bowl of kisses,
Should put your mouth to mine and drink of me.

Helen, you let my kisses steam
Wasteful into the night's black nostrils; drink
Me up, I pray; oh you, who are Night's bacchante,
How can you from my bowl of kisses shrink?

要求

你，海伦，把一颗颗星星看成
在黑树上燃烧的槲寄生果，
你一定把我当作亲吻之碗，
将嘴插入其中，吮吸着我。

海伦，你让我的亲吻白白地蒸发，
蒸进黑夜的鼻孔；把我吸光吧，我向你恳求；
哦，你呀，你这个夜间的狂饮作乐者，
面对我这亲吻之碗，你怎能缩脚缩手？

Silence

Since I lost you, I am silence-haunted;
　　Sounds wave their little wings
A moment, then in weariness settle
　　On the flood that soundless swings.

Whether the people in the street
　　Like pattering ripples go by,
Or whether the theatre sighs and sighs
　　With a loud, hoarse sigh:

Or the wind shakes a ravel of light
　　Over the dead-black river,
Or last night's echoing
　　Makes the daybreak shiver:

I feel the silence waiting
　　To take them all up again,
In its last completeness drinking
　　Down the noise of men.

寂静

自从我失去你，我就遭受寂静折磨，
　　声音将自己的羽翼挥动了一会儿，
随后便在疲惫中歇息下来，
　　歇息在一股无声旋动的洪波。

不知街头上来来去去的人们
　　是否步履轻快如同涟漪？
不知剧院里聚集一起的观众
　　是否发出响亮而嘶哑的叹息？

不知劲风是否将一团光线
　　投射到死一般黑暗的河面？
不知最后一个夜晚的回声
　　是否使拂晓感到一丝震撼？

我感觉到寂静正在等待
　　再一次将万物全都战胜，
在它的最终的结尾动作中
　　饮尽人类的所有的噪声。

Listening

I listen to the stillness of you,

    My dear, among it all;

I feel your silence touch my words as I talk,

    And hold them in thrall.

My words fly off a forge

    The length of a spark;

I see the silence easily sip them

    Up in the dark.

The lark sings loud and glad,

    Yet I am not loth

That silence should take the song and the bird

    And lose them both.

A train goes roaring south,

    The steam-flag flying;

I see the stealthy shadow of silence

    Alongside going.

And off the forge of the world

    Whirling in the draught of life

倾听

在所有的声音中，亲爱的，
　　我倾听来自你的寂静声息；
每当我开口，我就感觉到
　　你的寂静俘获了我的话语。

我的话语从熔炉之中
　　只是飞出了零星碎片，
我见到寂静轻而易举地
　　将我的话语吸进一片黑暗。

云雀的歌唱响亮又欢畅，
　　但是我宁愿寂静出面
攻克鸟儿以及鸟儿的歌声，
　　让它们不再呈现。

一列火车呼啸着奔向南方，
　　冒出的蒸气如飘荡的旗帜，
我看见寂静的秘密的身影
　　沿着道路挺进，寸步不离。

于是从世界的熔炉之中
　　冒出无数人们的言语火星，

Go myriad sparks of people, filling

    The night with strife.

Yet they never change the darkness

    Nor blench it with noise;

Alone on the perfect silence

    The stars are buoys.

在生命的气流中旋转，

　　奋力填充夜晚的空洞。

然而它们无法改变黑暗，

　　或者以声音让其退缩；

在一片完美的寂静之中，

　　唯一的浮标便是星辰闪烁。

Last Words to Miriam

Yours is the sullen sorrow,
  The disgrace is also mine;
Your love was intense and thorough,
Mine was the love of a growing flower
    For the sunshine.

You had the power to explore me,
  Blossom me stalk by stalk;
You woke my spirit, you bore me
To consciousness, you gave me the dour
    Awareness—then I suffered a balk.

Body to body I could not
  Love you, although I would.
We kissed, we kissed though we should not.
You yielded, we threw the last cast,
    And it was no good.

You only endured, and it broke
  My craftsman's nerve.
No flesh responded to my stroke;
So I failed to give you the last
    Fine torture you did deserve.

致米莉娅姆的最后的话语

你的遗憾之中带有愠怒，
　　蒙受的耻辱也是我的耻辱，
你的爱情无所畏惧，炽热强烈，
我的爱情是生长着的花朵，
　　对阳光情真意切。

你曾有对我进行探测的力量，
　　使我一枝一叶繁盛兴旺；
你唤醒了我的灵魂，你生育了我的意识，
你给了我阴郁的清醒——
　　然后，我遭受失利。

身体挨着身体与你相恋
　　我却不能，尽管情愿。
虽说不该，我们却不停地狂吻。
你一味地屈从，我们攻克了最后的堡垒，
　　可是没有特别的温存。

你只是忍受，这差不多炸崩
　　我这个名匠的神经。
没有肉体回答我的抚摩；
于是我放弃了向你赠送
　　你应受的甜蜜的折磨。

You are shapely, you are adorned
    But opaque and null in the flesh;
Who, had I but pierced with the thorned
Full anguish, perhaps had been cast
    In a lovely illumined mesh

Like a painted window; the best
    Fire passed through your flesh,
Undrossed it, and left it blest
In clean new awareness. But now
    Who shall take you afresh?

Now who will burn you free
    From your body's deadness and dross?
Since the fire has failed in me,
What man will stoop in your flesh to plough
    The shrieking cross?

A mute, nearly beautiful thing
    Is your face, that fills me with shame
As I see it hardening;
I should have been cruel enough to bring
    You through the flame.

你现在描饰得熠熠生辉，美丽匀称，
　　但肉体上却反应迟钝；
假若我被布满荆棘的苦恼
刺穿，那你也许已被抛进
　　可爱的明亮的圈套。

如颜色瑰丽的窗户；最好的火焰
　　会在你肉体上蔓延，
清除其中的杂质，使之得到净化，
获得新的纯洁的意识，但现在
　　谁会把你重新接纳？

现在，谁会燃烧你的身体，
　　除却其中的死寂与杂质？
既然在我身上火焰已熄，
哪个男人会屈尊地在你体内
　　耕犁发出尖叫的"十字"？

你脸蛋缄默不语，几乎能算美丽，
　　我觉得身上被它填满羞耻，
当我看到这张阴沉的脸，
我真该变得残酷无情，
　　拖曳着你去穿越火焰。

Snap-Dragon

She bade me follow to her garden, where
The mellow sunlight stood as in a cup
Between the old grey walls; I did not dare
To raise my face, I did not dare look up,
Lest her bright eyes like sparrows should fly in
My windows of discovery, and shrill "Sin!"

So with a downcast mien and laughing voice
I followed, followed the swing of her white dress
That rocked in a lilt along; I watched the poise
Of her feet as they flew for a space, then paused to press
The grass deep down with the royal burden of her;
And gladly I'd offered my breast to the tread of her.

"I like to see," she said, and she crouched her down,
She sunk into my sight like a settling bird;
And her bosom couched in the confines of her gown
Like heavy birds at rest there, softly stirred
By her measured breaths: "I like to see," said she,
"The snap-dragon put out his tongue at me."

She laughed, she reached her hand out to the flower,
Closing its crimson throat. My own throat in her power—

金鱼草

她邀我跟随她来到花园，
园中注满了柔和的阳光，
两边是灰色的古墙；我不敢
抬起眼睛，也不敢昂起脸膛，
唯恐她明亮的眼睛像两只麻雀
尖叫着："罪孽！"飞入我意识之窗。

于是我以垂头丧气的神态，
笑着跟随她白色衣裙的摇摆；
白裙节奏轻快地飘拂，
我观看她轻盈如飞的步态，
她停了下来，以高贵的重负把青草紧压；
我多想奉献出胸膛供她的纤足踩踏。

"我喜爱观望，"她说，并蹲下身子，
像一只栖息的小鸟映入我的眼帘；
她的乳房沉睡在外衣的边境，
像两只体重的鸟儿在那里安眠，
并且柔和地颤动，伴随她呼吸的节奏，
"我喜爱观望金鱼草向我伸出舌头。"

她笑逐颜开地把手伸向花朵，
贴近它绯红的咽喉。她的力量

Strangled, my heart swelled up so full
As if it would burst its wine-skin in my throat,
Choke me in my own crimson. I watched her pull
The gorge of the gaping flower, till the blood did float

Over my eyes, and I was blind—
Her large brown hand stretched over
The windows of my mind;
And there in the dark I did discover
Things I was out to find:

My Grail, a brown bowl twined
With swollen veins that met in the wrist,
Under whose brown the amethyst
I longed to taste! I longed to turn
My heart's red measure in her cup;
I longed to feel my hot blood burn
With the amethyst in her cup.

Then suddenly she looked up,
And I was blind in a tawny-gold day.
Till she took her eyes away.

也扼住我的喉咙，我的心脏无限地增大，
仿佛要胀破喉中的皮制酒囊，
把我窒息在自己的绯红之中。我观看她
撕摘张嘴花朵的咽喉，直至鲜血直淌，

在我眼前浮动，弄瞎我的双目，
她偌大的褐色手臂
伸展在我心灵的窗户；
在一片黑暗中我确实
发现了我所寻之物：

我的圣杯，一只褐色的酒杯，[1]
布满鼓胀的、在腕部交会的血管，
在这褐色的下面，是我渴求品尝的
紫水晶！我渴望在她杯中旋转
我心脏的红色量具；
我渴望感觉到在她杯里
我的热血伴随紫水晶熊熊燃起。

然后她突然昂起头来，
在金黄的日子！我耳鸣眼瞎，
直到她移开双眼。

1　圣杯（Grail）：耶稣在最后的晚餐时所用的杯，寓指长期以来梦寐以求的东西。

So she came down from above
And emptied my heart of love.
So I held my heart aloft
To the cuckoo that hung like a dove,
And she settled soft.

It seemed that I and the morning world
Were pressed cup-shape to take this reiver
Bird who was weary to have furled
Her wings in us,
As we were weary to receive her.

This bird, this rich,
Sumptuous central grain;
This mutable witch,
This one refrain,
This laugh in the fight,
This clot of night,
This field of delight.

She spoke, and I closed my eyes
To shut hallucinations out.
I echoed with surprise
Hearing my mere lips shout
The answer they did devise.

于是，她从上面走下，
吸空我的爱情之心。
所以我高高举起心脏
面对鸽子般悬着的杜鹃，
她轻柔地落在我的心上。

看来，我与这个凌晨世界
被压成杯子的形状，
来接待这只劫掠之鸟，
她讨厌将双翼收拢在我们身上，
如同我们对于接待她而感到厌烦。

　　这只鸟儿，这丰富、
　　豪华、集中的谷物，
　　这反复无常的女巫，
　　这一乐曲的叠句，
　　这战斗中的笑语，
　　这夜晚的一群，
　　这欢乐的园地。

她说起话来，我闭上眼睛，
从视野中驱走一群虚幻。
当我听见只有我的双唇，
呼喊出他们设想的答案，
我惊奇地发出回声。

Again I saw a brown bird hover

Over the flowers at my feet;

I felt a brown bird hover

Over my heart, and sweet

Its shadow lay on my heart.

I thought I saw on the clover

A brown bee pulling apart

The closed flesh of the clover

And burrowing in its heart.

She moved her hand, and again

I felt the brown bird cover

My heart; and then

The bird came down on my heart,

As on a nest the rover

Cuckoo comes, and shoves over

The brim each careful part

Of love, takes possession, and settles her down,

With her wings and her feathers to drown

The nest in a heat of love.

She turned her flushed face to me for the glint

Of a moment.—"See," she laughed, "if you also

Can make them yawn!" —I put my hand to the dint

In the flower's throat, and the flower gaped wide with woe.

我又看见一只褐色鸟儿
在我脚边的花朵上盘旋；
我感觉到一只褐色鸟儿
在我的心口起舞翩翩，
甜蜜的影子投在我心间。
我想我看到在三叶草上
一只黄色的蜜蜂撕开
三叶草的关闭的肌肤，
钻进它心中躲藏起来。

她移动纤手，我再次，
感觉到褐色鸟儿盖住
我的心房，然后，
鸟儿来到我心上，恰如
漫游归来的杜鹃落到鸟巢，
在边缘上，强硬推开
各个谨慎的爱情部位，
占领地域，定居下来，
以她的双翼和满身羽毛
淹没炽热爱情的小巢。

她向我转过绯红的脸，闪现出
瞬间的光芒。"看吧，"她笑着说，"看你
是否也能使它们张口打起呵欠！"我把手
放到那朵花儿喉咙的陷痕，花儿悲哀地张开裂口。

She watched, she went of a sudden intensely still,
She watched my hand, to see what it would fulfil.

I pressed the wretched, throttled flower between
My fingers, till its head lay back, its fangs
Poised at her. Like a weapon my hand was white and keen,
And I held the choked flower-serpent in its pangs
Of mordant anguish, till she ceased to laugh,
Until her pride's flag, smitten, cleaved down to the staff.

She hid her face, she murmured between her lips
The low word "Don't!" —I let the flower fall,
But held my hand afloat towards the slips
Of blossom she fingered, and my fingers all
Put forth to her: she did not move, nor I,
For my hand like a snake watched hers, that could not fly.

Then I laughed in the dark of my heart, I did exult
Like a sudden chuckling of music. I bade her eyes
Meet mine, I opened her helpless eyes to consult
Their fear, their shame, their joy that underlies
Defeat in such a battle. In the dark of her eyes
My heart was fierce to make her laughter rise.

她凝眸注视，突然强烈地静息下来，
她观看我的手，看她能够满足什么样的要求。

我把不幸的、脖子被掐的花朵夹在
我手指之间，直到它的脑袋朝后躺下，
尖顶朝地悬着。我的手如同武器，
光洁锐利，使窒息的蜿蜒的花
发出阵阵剧痛，直至她停止笑声，
她高傲之旗遭受袭击，撕裂，倒塌。

她藏起脸庞，两片嘴唇之间发出
喃喃的声音："不要这样！"我让花儿落地，
但是手儿慢悠悠地移向
她触碰之花的细茎，我的手指
全部伸向她：她没有动弹，我也没动，
因为我的手像蛇一样对她无法飞走的手进行监视。

然后我在心灵的黑暗深处发出笑声，我欢跃，
像突然击响的音乐之声。我吩咐她的眼睛
与我双眼相遇，我打开她无望的眼睛察看
它们的恐惧，羞耻，以及战败之下的欣幸。
在她眼睛的乌黑的深处，
我的心强烈地唤起她的笑声。

Till her dark deeps shook with convulsive thrills, and the dark

Of her spirit wavered like water thrilled with light;

And my heart leaped up in longing to plunge its stark

Fervour within the pool of her twilight,

Within her spacious soul, to find delight.

And I do not care, though the large hands of revenge

Shall get my throat at last, shall get it soon,

If the joy that they are lifted to avenge

Have risen red on my night as a harvest moon,

Which even death can only put out for me;

And death, I know, is better than not-to-be.

直至她的黑暗深处发出阵阵震颤，

她黑暗的心灵闪烁光泽，

像湖面上曳动着光线，

我的心跳跃起来，渴望把赤裸裸的炽热

投进她曙光初照的池塘，

投进它宽阔的灵魂，寻觅快乐。

尽管巨大的复仇之手最终会掐住我的喉咙，

很快就会掐住，但我毫不顾及

双手举起复仇的欢乐会像一轮圆月，

鲜红地升起在我的夜里。

唯有死亡才能为我将它熄灭；

但我知道，世间的死亡胜于不降临尘世。

A Love Song

Reject me not if I should say to you
I do forget the sounding of your voice,
I do forget your eyes, that searching through
The days perceive our marriage, and rejoice.

But, when the apple-blossom opens wide
Under the pallid moonlight's fingering,
I see your blanched face at my breast, and hide
My eyes from duteous work, malingering.

Ah, then upon the bedroom I do draw
The blind to hide the garden, where the moon
Enjoys the open blossoms as they straw
Their beauty for his taking, boon for boon.

And I do lift my aching arms to you,
And I do lift my anguished, avid breast,
And I do weep for very pain of you,
And fling myself at the doors of sleep, for rest.

And I do toss through the troubled night for you,
Dreaming your yielded mouth is given to mine,
Feeling your strong breast carry me on into
The sleep no dream nor doubt can undermine.

情歌

不要拒绝我，假若我对你说
我一定忘却你说话的声音，
我一定忘却你的眼睛，尽管多日以来，
它们观察我们的婚姻与欢欣。

但是，在一片皎洁的月光之下，
当苹果花儿漫山遍野地绽开，
我会看见你白净的脸蛋偎在我胸口，
我双眼不再忠于职守，开起小差。

哎，然后在卧室附近，我一定拉上窗帘
遮住花园，园中的月亮尽情享受
绽开的花朵，当花儿播撒着美色，
为了被月亮索取，为了方便月亮的请求。

我一定向你伸出疼痛的双臂，
我一定昂起苦恼的、热望的胸膛，
我一定为你的痛苦而悲泣，
一头扑进沉睡大门，为了安详。

在烦恼的夜晚，我一定为你辗转反侧，
幻想你屈服了的樱唇凑到我的嘴边，
觉得你强健的乳房把我带进
无论梦幻还是怀疑都无法打扰的睡眠。

Call into Death

Since I lost you, my darling, the sky has come near,
And I am of it, the small sharp stars are quite near,
The white moon going among them like a white bird
    among snow-berries,
And the sound of her gently rustling in heaven like a bird I hear.

And I am willing to come to you now, my dear,
As a pigeon lets itself off from a cathedral dome
To be lost in the haze of the sky; I would like to come
And be lost out of sight with you, like a melting foam.

For I am tired, my dear, and if I could lift my feet,
My tenacious feet, from off the dome of the earth
To fall like a breath within the breathing wind
Where you are lost, what rest, my love, what rest!

死亡的召唤

自我失去你，天空来到我跟前，
我在其中，耀眼的小星星就在身边，
苍白的月亮走在中间，像白色浆果之间的白鸟，
她的声音在空中轻柔作响，像我听到的鸟的鸣啭。

我情愿走到你的身边，我的亲人，
像一只鸽子飞离教堂的圆拱，
消失在朦胧的苍穹；我情愿向你投奔，
与你一起从视野消失，像泡沫一般消融。

我疲惫不堪，亲爱的，我多想提起我的双脚，
拖不动的双脚，离开地球的圆顶，
把我尚存的生命，我的爱人，抛落到
你消失之地，像轻风中的呼吸一声！

Piano

Softly, in the dusk, a woman is singing to me;

Taking me back down the vista of years, till I see

A child sitting under the piano, in the boom of the tingling strings

And pressing the small, poised feet of a mother who smiles

    as she sings.

In spite of myself, the insidious mastery of song

Betrays me back, till the heart of me weeps to belong

To the old Sunday evenings at home, with winter outside

And hymns in the cosy parlour, the tinkling piano our guide.

So now it is vain for the singer to burst into clamour

With the great black piano appassionato. The glamour

Of childish days is upon me, my manhood is cast

Down in the flood of remembrance, I weep like a child for

    the past.

钢琴

黄昏中，一个女人对我轻柔地歌唱，
引起我对往事的追忆，我看到
一个孩子坐在钢琴下，在清脆的旋律中，
触摸且唱且笑的母亲放平的小脚。

我不由自主，被歌的巨大魔力召回到过去，
我心中哭着想起家中的周末夜晚，
叮当的琴声引导我们唱着圣歌，
屋外一片隆冬，客厅里舒适温暖。

现在，歌者放声高唱只是枉然，
黑色大钢琴的狂奏也不再使我动心，
儿时的异彩占据了我，成年被回忆的洪流
冲毁，我思念过去，哭得像个幼婴。

On the Balcony

In front of the sombre mountains, a faint, lost ribbon of rainbow;
And between us and it, the thunder;
And down below in the green wheat, the labourers
Stand like dark stumps, still in the green wheat.

You are near to me, and your naked feet in their sandals,
And through the scent of the balcony's naked timber
I distinguish the scent of your hair: so now the limber
Lightning falls from heaven.

Adown the pale-green glacier river floats
A dark boat through the gloom——and whither?
The thunder roars. But still we have each other!
The naked lightnings in the heavens dither
And disappear——what have we but each other?
The boat has gone.

在阳台上

在幽暗的山前，有一条淡淡的、毁损的彩虹；
在我们与彩虹之间，是滚滚的雷鸣；
下方，青幽幽的麦田里站着农民，
像黑黝黝的树桩，静静地站在青幽幽的麦田。

你在我身边，赤足穿着凉鞋，
透过阳台上赤裸裸木材的芬芳
我辨别出你的发香；即刻，
迅速的闪电划破长空。

沿着淡绿的冰河，一艘黑色的船
漂过昏暗——又去何方？
雷声轰鸣。然而你有我，我有你！
赤裸裸的闪电在天空中战栗
并且消失——除了我有你、你有我，还有什么？
黑船已经漂走。

In the Dark

A blotch of pallor stirs beneath the high
Square picture-dusk, the window of dark sky.

A sound subdued in the darkness: tears!
As if a bird in difficulty up the valley steers.

"Why have you gone to the window? Why don't you sleep?
How you have wakened me! But why, why do you weep?"

"I am afraid of you, I am afraid, afraid!
There is something in you destroys me——!"

"You have dreamed and are not awake, come here to me."
"No, I have wakened. It is you, you are cruel to me!"

"My dear!"——"Yes, yes, you are cruel to me. You cast
A shadow over my breasts that will kill me at last."

"Come!"——"No, I'm a thing of life. I give
You armfuls of sunshine, and you won't let me live."

"Nay, I'm too sleepy!"——"Ah, you are horrible;
You stand before me like ghosts, like a darkness upright."

在黑暗中

在方形图画般的薄暮下面，
一个苍白的斑点游动在夜空的窗畔。

黑暗中传出压低的声乐：哭泣！
仿佛鸟雀艰难地朝山谷飞驶。

"你为何走到窗口？你为何不睡？
你把我惊醒了！可是，你干吗流泪？"

"我怕你，我惶恐，我惊骇！
你身上有什么东西把我毁坏——！"

"你未从梦中醒来，快向我靠近。"
"不，我已经睡醒。是你，是你待我残忍！"

"天哪！"——"是的，你待我残忍。你在我胸怀
投下一道阴影，它最终将把我杀害。"

"来吧！"——"不，我是一个性命。
我给你一抱阳光，你却不让我生存。"

"嗨，我太困了！"——"哎，你可怖万分；
你站在我面前，如同直立的黑暗，如同幽灵。"

"I!"—"How can you treat me so, and love me?
My feet have no hold, you take the sky from above me."

"My dear, the night is soft and eternal, no doubt
You love it!"—"It is dark, it kills me, I am put out."

"My dear, when you cross the street in the sunshine, surely
Your own small night goes with you. Why treat it so poorly?"

"No, no, I dance in the sun, I'm a thing of life—"
"Even then it is dark behind you. Turn round, my wife."

"No, how cruel you are, you people the sunshine
With shadows!"—"With yours I people the sunshine, yours
    and mine—"

"In the darkness we all are gone, we are gone with the trees
And the restless river;—we are lost and gone with all these."

"But I am myself, I have nothing to do with these."
"Come back to bed, let us sleep on our mysteries.

"Come to me here, and lay your body by mine,
And I will be all the shadow, you the shine.

"我？！"——"你怎能这样待我，这样爱我？
我无地立足，头上的天空也被你捕获。"

"亲爱的，你柔和的夜晚永生不死，
你一定爱它！"——"这黑夜把我杀害，把我吞噬。"

"亲爱的，当你在阳光下穿越大街，
你自身的黑夜一定与你紧随。你为何把它虐待？"

"不，不，我在阳光之中舞蹈，我是一个生命——"
"那你身后也仍有黑暗。我的妻子，请你转身。"

"不，你多么残忍，你是带着阴影的阳光！"
"我确实是阳光，把你我阴影带在身上——"

"在黑暗中我们全都消亡，随同树木
和永无休止的河流；——我们全都失落，随同这些
　　事物。"

"但我仍是我自己，我与这些东西毫不相干。"
"回来吧，让我们在神秘中躺在床上。

"回到我这儿，把你身子躺在我身边，
我愿做阴影，让你成为光线。

"Come, you are cold, the night has frightened you.

Hark at the river! It pants as it hurries through

"The pine-woods. How I love them so, in their mystery of

    not-to-be."

"—But let me be myself, not a river or a tree."

"Kiss me! How cold you are!—Your little breasts

Are bubbles of ice. Kiss me!—You know how it rests

"One to be quenched, to be given up, to be gone in the dark;

To be blown out, to let night dowse the spark.

"But never mind, my love. Nothing matters, save sleep;

Save you, and me, and sleep; all the rest will keep."

"回来吧，你身上寒冷，黑夜使你心胆俱裂。
听着小溪的声音！它气喘吁吁，当它匆忙穿越

"松树林。我爱松树，爱它无形的神秘。"
"——让我成为我自己，不是松树或一条小溪。"

"吻我吧！你身上多么寒冷！——你小小的乳房
如同冰块。吻我吧！你知道这一记亲吻的分量——

"被爱淹灭，降服，在黑暗中消亡，
被感情吹熄，让黑夜浸湿火光。

"但是不必介意，我的爱人。没有关系，除了睡眠；
除了你我，除了睡眠；其余一切依旧安然。"

Green

The dawn was apple-green,
    The sky was green wine held up in the sun,
The moon was a golden petal between.

She opened her eyes, and green
    They shone, clear like flowers undone
For the first time, now for the first time seen.

绿

黎明是一片苹果绿，
　　天空是举起在太阳下的绿酒；
月亮是两者间的金色的花瓣。

她睁开眼睛，射出
　　绿色光彩，纯净灵秀
像初绽的鲜花，此刻被人发现。

River Roses

By the Isar, in the twilight
We were wandering and singing,
By the Isar, in the evening
We climbed the huntsman's ladder and sat swinging
In the fir tree overlooking the marshes,
While river met with river, and the ringing
Of their pale-green glacier water filled the evening.

By the Isar, in the twilight
We found the dark wild roses
Hanging red at the river; and simmering
Frogs were singing, and over the river closes
Was savour of ice and of roses; and glimmering
Fear was abroad. We whispered: "No one knows us.
Let it be as the snake disposes
Here in this simmering marsh."

河边的蔷薇

在伊萨尔河畔的暮色之中，
我们一边歌唱一边漫步。
在伊萨尔河畔的黄昏之中，
我们沿着猎人的梯子攀登，
摇摇晃晃地坐在杉树枝头，俯瞰沼泽，
河流与河流交汇，浅绿色的冰冷的河水
用清脆的歌声填满了黄昏。

在伊萨尔河畔的暮色之中，
我们发现了深色的野蔷薇
红彤彤地悬挂在河畔，
骚动的青蛙放声歌唱，
河流交汇处的冰水中迷漫着蔷薇的香味；
微弱的畏惧掠过心头。我们喃喃自语：
"没有人认识我们。如同一条蛇，
被安置在处于骚动状态的沼泽。"

Gloire de Dijon

When she rises in the morning
I linger to watch her;
She spreads the bath-cloth underneath the window
And the sunbeams catch her
Glistening white on the shoulders,
While down her sides the mellow
Golden shadow glows as
She stoops to the sponge, and her swung breasts
Sway like full-blown yellow
Gloire de Dijon roses.

She drips herself with water, and her shoulders
Glisten as silver, they crumple up
Like wet and falling roses, and I listen
For the sluicing of their rain-dishevelled petals.
In the window full of sunlight
Concentrates her golden shadow
Fold on fold, until it glows as
Mellow as the glory roses.

壮丽的黄玫瑰

当她凌晨起床的时候，
我驻足对她凝望；
她拉上窗下的浴帘，
一束束阳光将她捕获，
在她的肩膀上熠熠发亮，
在她的两侧，闪烁着
金色的柔美的影像，
她俯身擦拭身体，
一对乳房晃动着，
如同两朵盛开的壮丽的黄玫瑰。

她将水淋在自己身上，她的双肩
闪着银光，并且起皱，
如同有点下垂的湿玫瑰。我倾听
因水而凌乱的花瓣发出的窸窣声音。
在洒满阳光的窗前，
她的金色身影凝聚，
层层相叠，闪烁光彩，
美得如同那壮丽的玫瑰。

Roses on the Breakfast Table

Just a few of the roses we gathered from the Isar
Are fallen, and their mauve-red petals on the cloth
Float like boats on a river, while other
Roses are ready to fall, reluctant and loth.

She laughs at me across the table, saying
I am beautiful. I look at the rumpled young roses
And suddenly realize, in them as in me,
How lovely is the self this day discloses.

餐桌上的蔷薇

从伊萨尔河畔采摘的几朵蔷薇
已经凋谢，紫红色的花瓣落在桌布上面，
如同帆船漂浮在河中，还有几朵
也即将凋谢，尽管很不情愿。

她从桌子对面朝我微笑，说我英俊，
我看着长有多重花瓣的鲜艳的蔷薇，
突然意识到我的情形如玫瑰一般，
这一天充分显示，当下何等优美！

Meeting among the Mountains

The little pansies by the road have turned
Away their purple faces and their gold,
And evening has taken all the bees from the thyme,
And all the scent is shed away by the cold.

Against the hard and pale blue evening sky
The mountain's new-dropped summer snow is clear
Glistening in steadfast stillness: like transcendent
Clean pain sending on us a chill down here.

Christ on the Cross!—his beautiful young man's body
Has fallen dead upon the nails, and hangs
White and loose at last, with all the pain
Drawn on his mouth, eyes broken at last by his pangs.

And slowly down the mountain road, belated,
A bullock wagon comes; so I am ashamed
To gaze any more at the Christ, whom the mountain snows
Whitely confront; I wait on the grass, am lamed.

The breath of the bullock stains the hard, chill air,
The band is across its brow, and it scarcely seems
To draw the load, so still and slow it moves,
While the driver on the shaft sits crouched in dreams.

相遇在山区

路边娇小的三色紫罗兰
转过紫红和金黄的脸庞，
暮色从麝香草上带走了所有的蜜蜂，
寒冷驱除了所有的芬芳。

与阴沉、淡蓝的夜空形成反衬，
高山上新降的夏雪洁白清晰，
在稳定的寂静中晶莹闪烁：像超常的
洁净的痛苦朝我们送来阵阵寒气。

基督钉在十字架上！——他年轻美男子的躯体
已经死在钉上，终于悬挂起来，
灰白、松弛，全部的疼痛
移到嘴上，双眼被剧痛劈开。

一辆姗姗来迟的牛车，沿着山路
慢悠悠地行驶；我感到羞耻，
不再观看与山上白雪相对的基督。
我提不起双足，等待在草地。

牛的呼吸玷污了硬性的、凉爽的空气，
辔头已经套上，牛车似乎
很难拖动如此重载，静静地、慢慢地移动，
而车杠上则蹲伏着已入梦境的车夫。

Surely about his sunburnt face is something
That vexes me with wonder. He sits so still
Here among all this silence, crouching forward,
Dreaming and letting the bullock take its will.

I stand aside on the grass to let them go;
—And Christ, I have met his accusing eyes again,
The brown eyes black with misery and hate, that look
Full in my own, and the torment starts again.

One moment the hate leaps at me standing there,
One moment I see the stillness of agony,
Something frozen in the silence that dare not be
Loosed, one moment the darkness frightens me.

Then among the averted pansies, beneath the high
White peaks of snow, at the foot of the sunken Christ
I stand in a chill of anguish, trying to say
The joy I bought was not too highly priced.

But he has gone, motionless, hating me,
Living as the mountains do, because they are strong,
With a pale, dead Christ on the crucifix of his heart,
And breathing the frozen memory of his wrong.

显然，关于这张晒黑的脸庞，
某种东西使我惊奇、烦恼。他寂然无息，
在一片寂静之中，朝前蹲伏着身体，
沉入梦境，让这头公牛自行其是。

我站在一旁的草地上让他们通过；
——还有基督，我又遇见他谴责的眼睛，
褐色的眼中含有深沉的痛苦和憎恨，
这种目光正对着我的双眼，折磨又开始产生。

有时，我站在那里，憎恨跳到我身上，
有时，我看到惨痛突发时的寂静，
冻结在不敢松懈的寂静中的东西，
有时，黑暗使我胆颤心惊。

然后，在转开脸的三色紫罗兰之间，在雪山陡峭的
白色山峰下面，在下陷的基督的脚下，
我恼怒地站着，浑身打颤，试图说出
我所买的欢乐并未付出昂贵的代价。

但他静静地走了，怀着对我的憎恨，
生活得如同崇山峻岭，因为它们坚毅，
苍白的、死亡的基督心口钉着十字架，
呼吸着他失误的冻结的记忆。

Still in his nostrils the frozen breath of despair,
And heart like a cross that bears dead agony
Of naked love, clenched in his fists the shame,
And in his belly the smouldering hate of me.

And I, as I stand in the cold, averted flowers,
Feel the shame-wounds in his hands pierce through my own,
And breathe despair that turns my lungs to stone
And know the dead Christ weighing on my bone.

然而在他鼻孔中仍有失望的冻结的呼吸，
心儿像十字架承受着裸体爱情的死寂的悲辛，
他的拳头中握紧了羞耻，
他的肚里闷烧着对我的满腔愤恨。

而我站在寒冷的、掉过脸的花朵之间，
感到他手上的羞辱之伤刺穿我的双手，
呼吸着把我双肺变成石头的失望，
知道死去的基督沉重地压着我的骨头。

Why Does She Weep?

Hush then
why do you cry?
It's you and me
the same as before.

If you hear a rustle
it's only a rabbit
gone back to his hole
in a bustle.

If something stirs in the branches
overhead, it will be a squirrel moving
uneasily, disturbed by the stress
of our loving.

Why should you cry then?
Are you afraid of God
in the dark?

I'm not afraid of God.
Let him come forth.
If he is hiding in the cover
let him come forth.

她为何哭叫？

那么你就安静下来，
你为何尖声哭叫？
还是我和你呀
和以前没有区别。

如果你听到了咝咝的声音，
那不过是一只兔子
匆匆忙忙地
返回它的洞中。

如果头上的树枝之间
有什么东西移动，那不过是
一只松鼠不安地跑动，
被我们的强烈的爱情所惊扰。

那么，你为何尖声哭叫？
你是因为害怕
黑暗之中的上帝？

我不害怕上帝，
让他走到跟前。
如果他藏在暗处，
让他露出真容。

Now in the cool of the day

it is we who walk in the trees

and call to God "Where art thou?"

And it is he who hides.

Why do you cry?

My heart is bitter.

Let God come forth to justify

himself now.

Why do you cry?

Is it Wehmut, ist dir weh?

Weep then, yea

for the abomination of our old righteousness.

We have done wrong

many times;

but this time we begin to do right.

Weep then, weep

for the abomination of our past righteousness.

God will keep

hidden, he won't come forth.

现在，在凉爽的白天，
是我们在林中散步，
高声对上帝说："你在哪里？"
是他藏在暗处。

你为何尖声哭叫？
我的心口疼痛。
让上帝露出真容，
前来证明自己。

你为何尖声哭叫？
是因为忧郁，而不是伤害？
那么，你就哭吧，
为了憎恨我们过去的正直。

我们曾经做过
许许多多错事，
但是这一回，我们开始走上正路。

哭吧，那么哭吧，
为了憎恨我们过去的正直。
上帝会继续隐藏，
他不会走到跟前。

Giorno dei Morti

Along the avenue of cypresses,

All in their scarlet cloaks and surplices

Of linen, go the chanting choristers,

The priests in gold and black, the villagers....

And all along the path to the cemetery

The round dark heads of men crowd silently,

And black-scarved faces of womenfolk, wistfully

Watch at the banner of death, and the mystery.

And at the foot of a grave a father stands

With sunken head, and forgotten, folded hands;

And at the foot of a grave a mother kneels

With pale shut face, nor either hears nor feels

The coming of the chanting choristers

Between the avenue of cypresses,

The silence of the many villagers,

The candle-flames beside the surplices.

万灵安魂曲

沿着松柏林荫大道，全都身披
红色斗篷或亚麻白色法衣，
走着唱圣歌的合唱队员、
村民以及红与黑的牧师……

全都沿着小径走向墓地，
男人的黑色圆头寂静地聚集，
女人的披着黑纱巾的脸面
愁闷地观看死亡之旗与神秘。

在一个坟脚站着一位父亲，
垂头丧气，神志恍惚，两手交叉，
在一个坟脚跪着一位母亲，
脸色惨白，两人都没听见或觉察

沿着松柏林荫大道，
唱着圣歌走来合唱队员，
众多的村民沉默不语，
烛光燃烧在白色法衣的旁边。

All Souls

They are chanting now the service of All the Dead
And the village folk outside in the burying ground
Listen—except those who strive with their dead,
Reaching out in anguish, yet unable quite to touch them:
Those villagers isolated at the grave
Where the candles burn in the daylight, and the painted wreaths
Are propped on end, there, where the mystery starts.

The naked candles burn on every grave.
On your grave, in England, the weeds grow.

But I am your naked candle burning,
And that is not your grave, in England,
The world is your grave.
And my naked body standing on your grave
Upright towards heaven is burning off to you
Its flame of life, now and always, till the end.

It is my offering to you; every day is All Souls' Day.

I forget you, have forgotten you.
I am busy only at my burning,

万灵节

他们现在为万灵节唱着圣歌
村民们在外面的墓地倾听——
除去爱与死者作对的人，村民们
悲痛地伸出手，可是无法触到死去的人；
那些村民在坟墓里离群索居，
蜡烛在日光中燃烧，色彩艳丽的花圈
挺直地置于涌出神秘的地方。

赤裸的蜡烛在每座坟冢上燃烧。
而在英格兰，在你的坟上，野草蔓生。

我就是你的燃烧着的裸体蜡烛，
可是在英格兰的坟冢不是你的，
世界才是你的坟冢。
我裸着身体站在你的坟上，
朝着苍天，始终向你燃出
生命的火焰，直至烧得精光。

这是我对你的献祭；每一天都是万灵节。

我忘却你，已经把你忘记。
我只是忙于燃烧自己，

I am busy only at my life.

But my feet are on your grave, planted.

And when I lift my face, it is a flame that goes up

To the other world, where you are now.

But I am not concerned with you.

I have forgotten you.

I am a naked candle burning on your grave.

我只是忙于奉献生命。

但我的双脚栽在你的坟上。

我昂起脸膛，那就是一股火焰，

升向你现在所住的另一个世界。

但是我与你没有关系。

　　我已经把你忘记。

我是一支在你坟上燃烧的裸体蜡烛。

December Night

Take off your cloak and your hat
And your shoes, and draw up at my hearth
Where never woman sat.

I have made the fire up bright;
Let us leave the rest in the dark
And sit by firelight.

The wine is warm in the hearth;
The flickers come and go.
I will warm your limbs with kisses
Until they glow.

十二月的夜晚

脱下你的斗篷，脱下你的鞋帽，
靠近我的炉边，
这儿从未有女人坐过。

我把炉火拨得辉煌；
让我们坐在火光旁边，
把其余沉入黑暗。

炉上的葡萄酒多么温暖，
火光摇曳，忽隐忽现。
我将以亲吻温暖你的四肢，
直至它们闪烁出光芒。

New Year's Eve

There are only two things now,
The great black night scooped out
And this fireglow.

This fireglow, the core,
And we the two ripe pips
That are held in store.

Listen, the darkness rings
As it circulates round our fire.
Take off your things.

Your shoulders, your bruised throat,
Your breasts, your nakedness!
This fiery coat!

As the darkness flickers and dips,
As the firelight falls and leaps
From your feet to your lips!

除夕

现在只剩下两件东西了，
一是凸现的恢宏的黑夜，
一是这灼热的炉火。

灼热的炉火，是核心，
而我们两个人
是储存其中的成熟的果仁。

请听，黑暗发出声响，
在炉火周围荡漾。
脱下你的衣裳。

你青肿的咽喉，你的肩膀，
你的赤裸，你的乳房！
你的外套也闪闪发光！

随着黑暗颤动、渗侵，
炉火的火光扑倒又欢腾，
从你的脚尖直到嘴唇！

Spring Morning

Ah, through the open door
Is there an almond tree
Aflame with blossom!
    —Let us fight no more.

Among the pink and blue
Of the sky and the almond flowers
A sparrow flutters.
    —We have come through,

It is really spring!—See,
When he thinks himself alone
How he bullies the flowers.
    —Ah, you and me

How happy we'll be!—See him?
He clouts the tufts of flowers
In his impudence.
    —But, did you dream

It would be so bitter? Never mind,
It is finished, the spring is here.

春天的早晨

透过敞开的大门，
可见一棵杏树
全身鲜花绽放！
　　——让我们不再争夺。

置身于朵朵粉红的杏花，
翱翔在一片蔚蓝的天边，
一只麻雀拍翅振翼。
　　——我们走过来了。

真的是春天来了！——看吧，
当他独自沉思，
他是如何欺侮鲜花。
　　——啊，你与我

将会多么幸福！——看见他啦？
他蛮横无耻地
猛烈袭击一束鲜花。
　　——但是，你是否梦见

这非常痛苦？不必介意，
事情已经结束，春天来到了这里。

And we're going to be summer-happy
    And summer-kind.

We have died, we have slain and been slain,
We are not our old selves any more.
I feel new and eager
    To start again.

It is gorgeous to live and forget.
And to feel quite new.
See the bird in the flowers?—he's making
    A rare to-do!

He thinks the whole blue sky
Is much less than the bit of blue egg
He's got in his nest—we'll be happy,
    You and I, I and you.

With nothing to fight any more—
In each other, at least.
See, how gorgeous the world is
    Outside the door!

我们将会像阳春一样愉快，[1]
　　——像阳春一样善良。

我们已经死亡，杀过人，也遭受了杀戮，
我们不再是过去的"我们"。
我感觉清新、渴望
　　重新开始一切。

生活和遗忘多么美好！
还有感觉清新。
看见杏花丛中的鸟雀吗？
　　他在制造稀有的骚扰！

他以为整个蓝空
比他巢中的蓝蛋
还要小得多——我们将会幸福，
　　你和我，我和你。

再也无物可争，
至少，在相互之间。
看吧，户外的世界
　　是多么地美好！

1　阳春：将 summer 译为"阳春"出于两种考虑：一是英国的夏天并不炎热；二是 summer 一词还可以用来与 winter 相对，表示"一年中较暖和的半年"。

History

The listless beauty of the hour
When snow fell on the apple trees
And the wood-ash gathered in the fire
And we faced our first miseries.

Then the sweeping sunshine of noon
When the mountains like chariot cars
Were ranked to blue battle—and you and I
Counted our scars.

And then in a strange, grey hour
We lay mouth to mouth, with your face
Under mine like a star on the lake,
And I covered the earth, and all space.

The silent, drifting hours
Of morn after morn
And night drifting up to the night
Yet no pathway worn.

Your life, and mine, my love
Passing on and on, the hate
Fusing closer and closer with love
Till at length they mate.

历史

此刻具有冷漠的美：
雪片落上了苹果树，
木灰聚集在火炉里，
我们面临初次的痛苦。

正午的阳光漫地扫射，
青山座座宛如战车一排，
列队进入蓝色的战场——你与我
数着我们的伤疤。

然后在奇特的灰色时刻，
我们唇贴唇地躺下，你的脸面
偎在我脸下，像湖面上的星，
我覆盖了大地，覆盖了全部空间。

寂静的、漂泊不定的时间，
从黎明向着黎明游漂，
从夜间又浮到夜间，
没有方向，没有目标。

你的生命，我的生命，
我的爱情不停地流逝，
憎恨与爱情亲密地融合，
直到最终结成一体。

Song of a Man Who Is Loved

Between her breasts is my home, between her breasts.
Three sides set on me space and fear, but the fourth side rests
Sure and a tower of strength, 'twixt the walls of her breasts.

Having known the world so long, I have never confessed
How it impresses me, how hard and compressed
Rocks seem, and earth, and air uneasy, and waters still ebbing west.

All things on the move, going their own little ways, and all
Jostling, people touching and talking and making small
Contacts and bouncing off again, bounce! bounce like a ball!

My flesh is weary with bounce and gone again!—
My ears are weary with words that bounce on them, and then
Bounce off again, meaning nothing. Assertions! Assertions!
    stones, women and men!

Between her breasts is my home, between her breasts.
Three sides set on me chaos and bounce, but the fourth side rests
Sure on a haven of peace, between the mounds of her breasts.

I am that I am, and no more than that: but so much
I am, nor will I be bounced out of it. So at last I touch
All that I am-not in softness, sweet softness, for she is such.

被恋者之歌

在她两个乳房之间是我的家，在她两个乳房之间。
我的家三面带来空白和恐惧，但是第四面
安稳地立着，像力量之塔，在她乳房的墙壁之间。

尽管老于世故，但我从来没有承认
它给我的印象该有多深，岩石凝缩、坚硬，
潮水向西边退落，土、气心神不定。

一切事物都在运动，走着自己的道路，
一切都在竞争，人们交谈、联系、接触，
又反跳而去，反跳！球一般地反跳而去！

我的肉体因反跳而疲倦，又一次虚弱无力！
我的耳朵也疲惫不堪，因为跳到耳上的话语
又反跳回去，毫无意义。那些主张、那些陈述！
　　那些宝石、男人和妇女！

在她两个乳房之间是我的家，在她两个乳房之间。
我的家三面带来混乱和弹跳，但是第四面
稳当地休息在宁静的避风港，在她小山般的乳房之间。

我就是我，就是如此；但是，即使如此，
我也不会被弹跳起来。于是我最后触击，
以甜蜜的温柔触击她这类非我所属的东西。

And the chaos that bounces and rattles like shrapnel, at least

Has for me a door into peace, warm dawn in the east

Where her bosom softens towards me, and the turmoil has ceased.

So I hope I shall spend eternity

With my face down buried between her breasts;

And my still heart full of security,

And my still hands full of her breasts.

像子弹一样弹跳、嗒嗒作响的混乱，对于我自己
至少是通往宁静的入口，东方温暖的晨曦
升了起来，她的胸怀朝我软化，骚动中止。

于是我希望度过永恒的时间，
在她的乳壕埋葬我的脸庞，
我宁静的心里充满了安全，
我宁静的双手充满了她的乳房。

Song of a Man Who Has Come Through

Not I, not I, but the wind that blows through me!
A fine wind is blowing the new direction of Time.
If only I let it bear me, carry me, if only it carry me!
If only I am sensitive, subtle, oh, delicate, a winged gift!
If only, most lovely of all, I yield myself and am borrowed
By the fine, fine wind that takes its course through the
    chaos of the world
Like a fine, an exquisite chisel, a wedge-blade inserted;
If only I am keen and hard like the sheer tip of a wedge
Driven by invisible blows,
The rock will split, we shall come at the wonder, we shall
    find the Hesperides.

Oh, for the wonder that bubbles into my soul,
I would be a good fountain, a good well-head,
Would blur no whisper, spoil no expression.

What is the knocking?
What is the knocking at the door in the night?
It is somebody wants to do us harm.

No, no, it is the three strange angels.
Admit them, admit them.

过来人之歌

不是我，而是风，穿过我的身体！
吹来一阵美妙的风，引导时光的方向。
但愿风儿能够将我吹起，将我带走！
但愿我能成为一件敏感的、微妙的、有翼的礼品！
但愿，我最期盼的，是让自己屈从，
出借给美妙的风，并按照风的路线行进，穿透世间的
　　混乱，
如同一柄利斧，或者一枚锐利的刀片。
假如我是锋利的刀刃
被无形的劲风所驱使，
我们定会劈开岩石，迎接奇迹，我们定会找到金苹果园。

哦，为了在我灵魂中激荡的奇迹，
我愿成为一湾清泉，成为美好的水源，
没有污染的噪音，没有毁损的表情。

哪里来的敲击声？
是谁在夜间的门上敲击？
有人想给我们带来伤害？

不是，不是。这是三位陌生的天使。
放他们进来，放他们进来。

Figs

The proper way to eat a fig, in society,

Is to split it in four, holding it by the stump,

And open it, so that it is a glittering, rosy, moist, honied,

     heavy-petalled four-petalled flower.

Then you throw away the skin

Which is just like a four-sepalled calyx,

After you have taken off the blossom with your lips.

But the vulgar way

Is just to put your mouth to the crack, and take out the flesh in one bite.

Every fruit has its secret.

The fig is a very secretive fruit.

As you see it standing growing, you feel at once it is symbolic:

And it seems male.

But when you come to know it better, you agree with the

     Romans, it is female.

The Italians vulgarly say, it stands for the female part; the fig-fruit:

The fissure, the yoni,

The wonderful moist conductivity towards the centre.

无花果

社会上，吃无花果的恰当方法，
就是把它放在树桩上，劈成四份，
把它打开，于是它就形成了放射光彩的、玫瑰色的、
　　含有水分的、甜如蜜的、花瓣沉重的四瓣花朵。

接着你用嘴唇吞下那朵花，
然后，你扔掉它的皮壳
这皮壳就像四片花萼。

但粗俗的方法，
就是用嘴哑开皮壳，一口取出果肉。

每一颗果实都有自己的秘密。

无花果是非常守密的果实。
当你看到它伫立成长时，你立刻感到它具有象征性。
它似乎是男性的。
但是，当你更进一步了解之后，你就会同意罗马人的
　　观点：它是女性的。

意大利人粗俗地说，它，无花果，代表女性的私处：
有裂缝，有通道，
有通往神经中枢的美好的湿性传导。

Involved,

Inturned,

The flowering all inward and womb-fibrilled;

And but one orifice.

The fig, the horse-shoe, the squash-blossom.

Symbols.

There was a flower that flowered inward, womb-ward;

Now there is a fruit like a ripe womb.

It was always a secret.

That's how it should be, the female should always be secret.

There never was any standing aloft and unfolded on a bough

Like other flowers, in a revelation of petals;

Silver-pink peach, venetian green glass of medlars and
  sorb-apples,

Shallow wine-cups on short, bulging stems

Openly pledging heaven:

Here's to the thorn in the flower! Here is to Utterance!

The brave, adventurous rosaceae.

Folded upon itself, and secret unutterable,

And milky-sapped, sap that curdles milk and makes ricotta,

包缠进去，

向内拐弯，

花朵全在内部开放，在有纤维组织的子宫内部，

但只有一个孔口。

无花果，马蹄形，压扁的花。

象征的符号。

有一朵花曾在内部，在子宫内部开放；

现在有了一颗果实，就像成熟的子宫。

它始终是个秘密。

事情就是这样，女性应该始终成为秘密。

无花果从未高高在上地站着，在树枝上开放，

像其他的花朵，展现出花瓣，

银白、粉红的桃子，威尼斯绿色玻璃器皿中的欧楂和

　　山梨，

杯脚短矮、膨胀的浅酒杯

直截了当地向上苍祝酒：

"为花朵中的荆棘干杯！为终极干杯！"

勇敢的、冒险的蔷薇。

自我交叠，秘密难以形容，

牛奶般的液汁，使牛奶凝结，制成乳酪，

Sap that smells strange on your fingers, that even goats won't
    taste it;
Folded upon itself, enclosed like any Mohammedan woman.
Its nakedness all within-walls, its flowering forever unseen,
One small way of access only, and this close-curtained from the light;
Fig, fruit of the female mystery, covert and inward,
Mediterranean fruit, with your covert nakedness,
Where everything happens invisible, flowering and fertilisation,
    and fruiting
In the inwardness of your you, that eye will never see
Till it's finished, and you're over-ripe, and you burst to give up
    your ghost.

Till the drop of ripeness exudes,
And the year is over.

And then the fig has kept her secret long enough.
So it explodes, and you see through the fissure the scarlet.
And the fig is finished, the year is over.

That's how the fig dies, showing her crimson through the
    purple slit
Like a wound, the exposure of her secret, on the open day.
Like a prostitute, the bursten fig, making a show of her secret.

That's how women die too.

这液汁在你手指间发出怪味，连山羊也不愿品尝；
自我交叠，就像任何伊斯兰教的妇女一样封闭起来。
它的裸露全在壁内，它的花朵永远不可目击，
只有一条狭窄的通路，而且已封闭遮光，
无花果，女性秘密之果，遮蔽在内部，
地中海的果实，你带着掩蔽的裸体，
在那儿，一切事情的发生都是不可见的，
　　开花、授粉、结果，
都发生在你的"你"的内部，眼睛怎么也看不见，
直到它完成，你过于成熟，突然绽开，泄露出你的幽灵。

待到成熟的汁向外渗出，
一个年头也就结束。

无花果已经将自己的秘密守了足够长的时间。
所以它破裂开来，于是你透过裂缝看到了鲜红。
无花果完结了，一年结束了。

无花果就是这样死亡，透过紫色的像伤口一样的裂缝，
来显露她的鲜红，在光天化日之下，暴露自己的秘密。
就像一名娼妓，绽开的无花果炫耀她的秘密。

女人也是这样死亡。

The year is fallen over-ripe,

The year of our women.

The year of our women is fallen over-ripe.

The secret is laid bare.

And rottenness soon sets in.

The year of our women is fallen over-ripe.

When Eve once knew in her mind that she was naked

She quickly sewed fig-leaves, and sewed the same for the man.

She'd been naked all her days before,

But till then, till that apple of knowledge, she hadn't had the

     fact on her mind.

She got the fact on her mind, and quickly sewed fig-leaves.

And women have been sewing ever since.

But now they stitch to adorn the bursten fig, not to cover it.

They have their nakedness more than ever on their mind,

And they won't let us forget it.

Now, the secret

Becomes an affirmation through moist, scarlet lips

That laugh at the Lord's indignation.

What then, good Lord! cry the women.

We have kept our secret long enough.

一个年头过于成熟了，

我们妇女的一年。

我们妇女的一年熟透了，

秘密无遮蔽地摆了出来，

腐烂立刻钻了进去。

我们妇女的年头熟透了。

当夏娃心中知道她是赤身裸体，

她马上用无花果树叶缝衣，也为亚当缝了一件。

以前，她一直赤身裸体，

但是，在她未吃知识果之前，她心中却全然不知。

她心中得知了这一事实，很快缝起了无花果树叶。

打那以后，女人就一直不停地缝制。

但是现在她们缝纫是为了装饰绽开的无花果，而不是把它

　　遮盖。

她们有着她们心中从未有过的那么多的赤裸，

她们还不愿让我们将此遗忘。

现在，那秘密

通过湿润的、鲜红的嘴唇得了证实，

这嘴唇嘲笑了上帝的义愤。

"那又怎样，老天爷？！"女人们嚷道。

"我们守密又守了足够的时间，

We are a ripe fig.

Let us burst into affirmation.

They forget, ripe figs won't keep.

Ripe figs won't keep.

Honey-white figs of the north, black figs with scarlet inside,

    of the south.

Ripe figs won't keep, won't keep in any clime.

What then, when women the world over have all bursten into

    self-assertion?

And bursten figs won't keep?

我们是成熟的无花果。
让我们绽开来证实秘密。”

她们忘了，成熟的无花果是留不住的。
成熟的无花果留不住。

北方的纯白的无花果，南方的里红外黑的无花果，
成熟的无花果留不住，任何地方也留不住。
那该怎么办，当全世界的妇女都突然绽开，自作主张？
绽开的无花果留不住吗？

Almond Blossom

Even iron can put forth,
Even iron.

This is the iron age,
But let us take heart
Seeing iron break and bud,
Seeing rusty iron puff with clouds of blossom.

The almond tree,
December's bare iron hooks sticking out of earth.

The almond tree,
That knows the deadliest poison, like a snake
In supreme bitterness.

Upon the iron, and upon the steel,
Odd flakes as if of snow, odd bits of snow,
Odd crumbs of melting snow.

But you mistake, it is not from the sky;
From out the iron, and from out the steel,
Flying not down from heaven, but storming up,
Strange storming up from the dense under-earth

杏花

甚至连钢铁也能开花，
甚至连钢铁。

这是铁器时期，
但是让我们鼓起勇气
看钢铁绽开，萌芽，
看生锈的钢铁喷放出束束鲜花。

杏树，
十二月的光秃的铁钩从土中戳出。

杏树，
它知道致命的毒物，像一条
极度痛苦中的蛇。

在铁的上面，在钢的上面，
生出奇特的雪片，零星的雪片，
少许正在融化的雪。

然而你弄错了，它不是来自苍穹；
而是来自铁，来自钢，
不是从天空飞下，而是从下方猛然冲出，
从愚钝的地下世界奇特地猛冲而出，

Along the iron, to the living steel

In rose-hot tips, and flakes of rose-pale snow

Setting supreme annunciation to the world.

Nay, what a heart of delicate super-faith,

Iron-breaking,

The rusty swords of almond trees.

Trees suffer, like races, down the long ages.

They wander and are exiled, they live in exile through

    long ages

Like drawn blades never sheathed, hacked and gone black,

The alien trees in alien lands: and yet

The heart of blossom,

The unquenchable heart of blossom!

Look at the many-cicatrised frail vine, none more scarred

    and frail,

Yet see him fling himself abroad in fresh abandon

From the small wound-stump.

Even the wilful, obstinate, gummy fig tree

Can be kept down, but he'll burst like a polyp into prolixity.

And the almond tree, in exile, in the iron age!

沿着铁，冲向活生生的钢，
在玫瑰般炽热的尖端，玫瑰般苍白的雪片
向世界作出最重要的通报。

哦，多么圣洁、优美的心，
铁的绽放，
杏树的生锈的剑。

树木像人类一样，在长久的世纪中遭难。
它们流浪、放逐，长期生活在流亡之中，
像拔出的永远无法入鞘的剑，砍劈，变黑，
异国的异树：然而是
鲜花的心脏，
鲜花的不可熄灭的心脏！

看看有许多疤痕的虚弱的葡萄树，谁也不会这么虚弱，
　　瘢痕累累，
可是你看它冲出小小的砍伤的树桩，
尽情地、生气勃然地冲向外部世界。

甚至连任性的、顽固的、多胶的无花果树
也能被砍倒，但它会像珊瑚虫，爆发成众多。

这杏树，在流放中，在铁器时代！

This is the ancient southern earth whence the vases were
    baked, amphoras, craters, cantharus, oenochoe, and
    open-hearted cylix,
Bristling now with the iron of almond trees.

Iron, but unforgotten.
Iron, dawn-hearted,
Ever-beating dawn-heart, enveloped in iron against the
    exile, against the ages.

See it come forth in blossom
From the snow-remembering heart
In long-nighted January,
In the long dark nights of the evening star, and Sirius, and
    the Etna snow-wind through the long night.

Sweating his drops of blood through the long-nighted
    Gethsemane
Into blossom, into pride, into honey-triumph, into most
    exquisite splendour.
Oh, give me the tree of life in blossom
And the Cross sprouting its superb and fearless flowers!

Something must be reassuring to the almond, in the evening
    star, and the snow-wind, and the long, long nights,

这是古代的南方黏土，曾烧成了坛坛罐罐，烧成了
　　花瓶，烧成了敞开心怀的高脚宽口酒杯，
现在却被杏树之铁密密覆盖。

铁，无法忘怀的铁。
铁，有醒悟之心的铁，
永远敲击的醒悟之心，包缠在铁中，反抗流放，反
　　抗时代。

看吧，它从对白雪记忆犹新的心中
以鲜花的形式涌出来，
在长夜漫漫的一月，
在有金星和天狼星的漫长的黑夜，在整夜怒吼的埃
　　特纳火山的风雪之中。

通过长夜漫漫的客西马尼园把他的血滴[1]
排进鲜花，排进自豪，排进如蜜的征服，排进最为
　　优雅的光彩。
哦，给我一棵鲜花盛开的生命之树，
给我一个绽放出无畏的壮丽鲜花的十字架！

某些事情必须再使杏树感到放心，在金星中，在风
　　雪里，在漫长漫长的夜晚，

1　客西马尼园：位于耶路撒冷附近，据传是耶稣被捕处。

Some memory of far, sun-gentler lands,

So that the faith in his heart smiles again

And his blood ripples with that untellable delight of once-
    more-vindicated faith,

And the Gethsemane blood at the iron pores unfolds, unfolds,

Pearls itself into tenderness of bud

And in a great and sacred forthcoming steps forth, steps
    out in one stride

A naked tree of blossom, like a bridegroom bathing in
    dew, divested of cover,

Frail-naked, utterly uncovered

To the green night-baying of the dog-star, Etna's snow-
    edged wind

And January's loud-seeming sun.

Think of it, from the iron fastness

Suddenly to dare to come out naked, in perfection of
    blossom, beyond the sword-rust.

Think, to stand there in full unfolded nudity, smiling,

With all the snow-wind, and the sun-glare, and the dog-
    star baying epithalamion.

Oh, honey-bodied beautiful one,

Come forth from iron,

Red your heart is.

某些对于遥远的、阳光柔和的大地的记忆，

好让它心中的信仰再次微笑，

它的血液中泛起不可言状的幸福涟漪，因为有了重
　　新辨明的信仰，

客西马尼园的血在铁孔中显露出来，显露出来，

珍珠般地滴进蓓蕾的温柔之中，

显著地、神圣地向前迈进，一步跨出

一棵裸体的花树，像一个新郎沐浴在晨露之中，脱
　　去了衣服，

少妇般的赤裸，完完全全的裸露，

面对天狼星的绿色的夜间吠叫，埃特纳火山的夹着
　　雪片的风，

和一月里的外表艳丽的太阳。

试想一下，从铁的坚固中，

突然敢于赤身裸体地出来，化为鲜花的优美，逃离
　　剑的铁锈。

试想一下，站在那里，以完全张开的裸露，笑容可掬，

伴着全部的风雪，炫目的阳光，天狼星吠唱的颂歌。

啊，躯体甜蜜的美人儿，

你从铁中跨出，

你的心是如此鲜红。

Fragile-tender, fragile-tender life-body,

More fearless than iron all the time,

And so much prouder, so disdainful of reluctances.

In the distance like hoar-frost, like silvery ghosts communing

    on a green hill,

Hoar-frost-like and mysterious.

In the garden raying out

With a body like spray, dawn-tender, and looking about

With such insuperable, subtly-smiling assurance,

Sword-blade-born.

Unpromised,

No bounds being set.

Flaked out and come unpromised,

The tree being life-divine,

Fearing nothing, life-blissful at the core

Within iron and earth.

Knots of pink, fish-silvery

In heaven, in blue, blue heaven,

Soundless, bliss-full, wide-rayed, honey-bodied,

Red at the core,

Red at the core,

Knotted in heaven upon the fine light.

柔嫩温顺，柔嫩温顺的生命，

始终比钢铁更坚强无畏，

更自豪骄傲，藐视阻抗。

在远方，如同白霜，如同在青山上沉思的银白的幽灵，

白霜一般，神秘无比。

在花园里放射出来，

带着曙光般柔和的犹如浪花的躯体，

环顾四周，以不可克制的、喜形于色的自信，

从刀剑中诞生。

没有诺言，

没有限制。

雪片般降世，毫无诺言地来临，

这杏树是神性的生命，

无所畏惧，在铁与土的核心

过着极乐的生活。

一簇簇粉红、银白，

在天空，在湛蓝湛蓝的天空，

没有声音，充满乐趣，光芒灿烂，躯体甜蜜，

核心是鲜红，

核心是鲜红，

在天空，在美丽的光线下，结成一簇一簇。

Open,

Open,

Five times wide open,

Six times wide open,

And given, and perfect;

And red at the core with the last sore-heartedness,

Sore-hearted-looking.

打开，

打开，

五倍地敞开，

六倍地敞开，

奉献，完善；

核心鲜红，伴有最后的痛苦的热忱，

外貌上的痛苦的热忱。

Snake

A snake came to my water-trough
On a hot, hot day, and I in pyjamas for the heat,
To drink there.

In the deep, strange-scented shade of the great dark carob tree
I came down the steps with my pitcher
And must wait, must stand and wait, for there he was at the
     trough before me.

He reached down from a fissure in the earth-wall in the gloom
And trailed his yellow-brown slackness soft-bellied down,
    over the edge of the stone trough
And rested his throat upon the stone bottom,
And where the water had dripped from the tap, in a small clearness,
He sipped with his straight mouth,
Softly drank through his straight gums, into his slack long body,
Silently.

Someone was before me at my water-trough,
And I, like a second comer, waiting.

He lifted his head from his drinking, as cattle do,
And looked at me vaguely, as drinking cattle do,
And flickered his two-forked tongue from his lips, and mused a moment,

蛇

气候炎热，我穿着睡衣，
一条蛇爬向我的水槽，
前去喝水。

在巨大的黑色角豆树的气味奇特的浓荫里，
我提着大水罐走下台阶，
必须等待，必须站住等待，因为他呆在我眼前的水槽边。

他从暗处土墙的裂缝中爬下，
拖曳着黄褐色的松弛的软肚子，来到石头水槽的边缘，
把喉咙搭在石槽底部休息。
那儿，水从龙头一点一点地清楚地滴下，
他用笔直的嘴啜饮着，
喝下的水通过笔直的牙床，舒畅地流入松弛的长长躯体，
静静地流入。

别人超前到了我的水槽，
我呀，像后来的人，等待着。

他从水槽抬起头来，就像一头牲口，
呆滞地盯着我，就像一头喝水的牲口，
从嘴里轻轻地弹出双叉舌头，沉思了一会儿，

And stooped and drank a little more,

Being earth-brown, earth-golden from the burning bowels

of the earth

On the day of Sicilian July, with Etna smoking.

The voice of my education said to me

He must be killed,

For in Sicily the black, black snakes are innocent, the gold

are venomous.

And voices in me said, If you were a man

You would take a stick and break him now, and finish him off.

But must I confess how I liked him,

How glad I was he had come like a guest in quiet, to drink

at my water-trough

And depart peaceful, pacified, and thankless,

Into the burning bowels of this earth?

Was it cowardice, that I dared not kill him?

Was it perversity, that I longed to talk to him?

Was it humility, to feel so honoured?

I felt so honoured.

And yet those voices:

If you were not afraid, you would kill him!

又俯身去喝了一点，
在这个西西里的七月的日子，当埃特纳火山仍旧冒烟
　　之时，
他像土地一样发褐，像土地一样金黄，
就像一根从大地的躯体中冒出来的燃烧的大肠。
我所受的教育发出声音，对我说：
必须处死他，
因为在西西里，黑色的蛇是清白的，金色的蛇是有毒的。

我身上的声音说，假若你是个男子汉，
你就该抓起棍棒，把他打断，把他打死。

但我必须承认，我非常喜欢他，
我格外高兴地看到他安静地来到这儿做客，
在我的水槽里喝水，然后平静地、温和地离开，
用不着道谢，回到大地躯体内其他燃烧的大肠中间。

是否出于懦弱，我不敢把他杀死？
是否出于堕落．我盼望与他交谈？
是否一种羞辱，我竟然感到光荣？
我感到如此光荣。

然而，又传出了声音：
"假若你不害怕，你就得把他处死！"

And truly I was afraid, I was most afraid,

But even so, honoured still more

That he should seek my hospitality

From out the dark door of the secret earth.

He drank enough

And lifted his head, dreamily, as one who has drunken,

And flickered his tongue like a forked night on the air, so black,

Seeming to lick his lips,

And looked around like a god, unseeing, into the air,

And slowly turned his head,

And slowly, very slowly, as if thrice adream,

Proceeded to draw his slow length curving round

And climb again the broken bank of my wall-face.

And as he put his head into that dreadful hole,

And as he slowly drew up, snake-easing his shoulders, and
    entered farther,

A sort of horror, a sort of protest against his withdrawing into
    that horrid black hole,

Deliberately going into the blackness, and slowly drawing
    himself after,

Overcame me now his back was turned.

I looked round, I put down my pitcher,

的确，我感到害怕，感到非常害怕，
即使如此，我更感到光荣，
因为他能从秘密大地的黑暗的门中走出，
前来寻求我的好客之情。

他喝足了，
神情恍惚地昂起头来，就像一名醉汉，
并且在空中摇动着他那叉状黑夜般的舌头，
似乎在舔着嘴唇，
接着像视而不见的神，环顾空中，
慢悠悠地转动脑袋，
慢悠悠地，慢悠悠地，仿佛耽于梦幻之中，
开始拖曳长长的、绕成曲线的躯体，
又爬上了破裂的墙面。

当他把脑袋伸进那可怕的洞穴，
当他慢慢地停住，放松肩膀，再继续进洞，
当他撤进那可怕的黑洞，不慌不忙地进入黑暗，
　　慢慢地把身子拖进去，
一种恐怖，一种对他这种行为的反抗，
占据了我的心身，可他对我不予理睬。

我环视四周，我放下水罐，

I picked up a clumsy log
And threw it at the water-trough with a clatter.

I think it did not hit him,
But suddenly that part of him that was left behind convulsed in
    undignified haste,
Writhed like lightning, and was gone
Into the black hole, the earth-lipped fissure in the wall-front,
At which, in the intense still noon, I stared with fascination.

And immediately I regretted it.
I thought how paltry, how vulgar, what a mean act!
I despised myself and the voices of my accursed human education.

And I thought of the albatross,
And I wished he would come back, my snake.

For he seemed to me again like a king,
Like a king in exile, uncrowned in the underworld,
Now due to be crowned again.

And so, I missed my chance with one of the lords
Of life.
And I have something to expiate:
A pettiness.

我捡起笨重的木头，

啪的一声砸向水槽。

我想我没有砸中他，

但是，他留在后面仓促地摆动着的部位

突然闪电般地蠕动了一下，

进入了黑洞，进入了墙面上的裂缝，

我带着迷恋凝视着黑洞，在这个酷热的宁静的中午。

我立刻感到懊悔。

我想到我的行动是多么粗暴，多么卑鄙！

我憎恨我自己，憎恨可恶的人类教育的声音。

我回想起了信天翁的故事。[1]

我希望他能够回来，我的蛇呀。

因为我又觉得他像一个皇帝，

像一个流放中的皇帝，废黜到了地狱，

他一定会马上重新戴上皇冠。

于是，我失去了一次与人生的君主

交往的机会。

我必将受到惩罚，

因为自己的卑劣。

---

1 指柯尔律治长诗《古舟子咏》中的信天翁的故事，水手杀死一只信天翁，结
果得到恶报。

Baby Tortoise

You know what it is to be born alone,
Baby tortoise!

The first day to heave your feet little by little from the shell,
Not yet awake,
And remain lapsed on earth,
Not quite alive.

A tiny, fragile, half-animate bean.

To open your tiny beak-mouth, that looks as if it would
    never open,
Like some iron door;
To lift the upper hawk-beak from the lower base
And reach your skinny little neck
And take your first bite at some dim bit of herbage,
Alone, small insect,
Tiny bright-eye,
Slow one.

To take your first solitary bite
And move on your slow, solitary hunt.
Your bright, dark little eye,

幼小的乌龟

幼小的乌龟啊，
你知道生来孤独是什么滋味！

第一天，渐渐将你的四脚从甲壳中伸出，
未等完全领悟，
便在世间堕落，
尚未真正成活。

一个幼小的、脆弱的、半死半活的小东西。

张开你的小嘴，它像一扇铁门，
仿佛永远不会开启；
从底部抬起你的上嘴唇，
伸出你的瘦得皮包骨的小脖子，
望着朦胧的牧草，生命中第一次觅食，
孤单的、无足轻重的小乌龟，
睁开明亮的小眼睛，
缓缓地移动。

生命中第一次孤单地觅食，
缓慢地前行，孤单地寻找。
你有明亮的乌黑的小眼睛，

Your eye of a dark disturbed night,
Under its slow lid, tiny baby tortoise,
So indomitable.

No one ever heard you complain.

You draw your head forward, slowly, from your little wimple
And set forward, slow-dragging, on your four-pinned toes,
Rowing slowly forward.
Whither away, small bird?
Rather like a baby working its limbs,
Except that you make slow, ageless progress
And a baby makes none.

The touch of sun excites you,
And the long ages, and the lingering chill
Make you pause to yawn,
Opening your impervious mouth,
Suddenly beak-shaped, and very wide, like some suddenly
        gaping pincers;
Soft red tongue, and hard thin gums,
Then close the wedge of your little mountain front,
Your face, baby tortoise.

你有如被惊扰的黑夜一般的眼睛，
幼小的乌龟啊，你缓缓移动在甲壳下方，
如此地不屈不挠。

无人听到你的抱怨的声音。

你从你的头巾中将脑袋向前伸出，
你用钉状的四脚缓缓地向前挺进，
慢悠悠地前行。
小东西，你究竟要去何方？
你更像在活动四肢的婴儿，
只不过你在永恒地缓慢行进，
而婴儿则不太活动。

阳光的抚摸让你激动，
长久的时代，逗留不去的寒意
让你停下来打个呵欠，
你于是张开密封的嘴，
突然变成喙状，相当宽阔，如同突然敞开的虎钳；
柔软的红舌头，坚硬的细齿龈，
幼小的乌龟啊，接着你就闭合
你山巅一般的楔形脸庞。

Do you wonder at the world, as slowly you turn your head
    in its wimple
And look with laconic, black eyes?
Or is sleep coming over you again,
The non-life?

You are so hard to wake.

Are you able to wonder?
Or is it just your indomitable will and pride of the first life
Looking round
And slowly pitching itself against the inertia
Which had seemed invincible?

The vast inanimate,
And the fine brilliance of your so tiny eye.
Challenger.

Nay, tiny shell-bird,
What a huge vast inanimate it is, that you must row against,
What an incalculable inertia.

Challenger,
Little Ulysses, fore-runner,

你是否对世界感到震惊，于是将脑袋缩进
　　　自己的头巾，
用一双精练的黑眼睛朝外观望？
或者是毫无生命迹象的睡眠
再一次侵入你的全身？

苏醒对于你极为艰难。

你是否能够感到震惊？
或者只是你坚强的意志和生存的自豪，
让你环顾四周之后，
又慢慢地俯仰
似乎难以攻克的惰性？

面对辽阔的死气沉沉，
你弱小的眼睛射出美妙的光泽。
一个挑战者。

然而，一只长着甲壳的小鸟
怎能面对如此辽阔的死气沉沉？
而且惰性又是如此难以估量。

一个挑战者。
小尤利西斯，一个先驱者，

No bigger than my thumb-nail,
Buon viaggio.

All animate creation on your shoulder,
Set forth, little Titan, under your battle-shield.

The ponderous, preponderate,
Inanimate universe;
And you are slowly moving, pioneer, you alone.

How vivid your travelling seems now, in the troubled sunshine,
Stoic, Ulyssean atom;
Suddenly hasty, reckless, on high toes.

Voiceless little bird,
Resting your head half out of your wimple
In the slow dignity of your eternal pause.
Alone, with no sense of being alone,
And hence six times more solitary;
Fulfilled of the slow passion of pitching through immemorial
    ages
Your little round house in the midst of chaos.

Over the garden earth,
Small bird,
Over the edge of all things.

比我的拇指甲也大不了多少，
旅途愉快。

所有生气勃勃的创造都在你的肩上，
前进，小提坦，在你的作战盔甲下前进。

在沉闷呆滞，又占有优势的、
单调枯燥的宇宙世界上；
先驱者啊，你缓缓地独自运动。

在纷扰的阳光下，你现在的旅行显得格外生动，
坚忍克己，含有尤利西斯元素；
突然间，昂起脚尖，不计后果地匆忙前行。

沉默无声的小鸟啊，
在永久停顿的缓慢的尊严中，
你把头半伸在头巾之外。
孑然一身，没有孤单的感觉，
因而具有六倍的孤单。
满怀穿越古老岁月的迟缓的激情，
你圆形的小屋置身于混乱。

在庭院的泥土上，
小小的鸟啊，
在一切事物的边缘。

Traveller,

With your tail tucked a little on one side

Like a gentleman in a long-skirted coat.

All life carried on your shoulder,

Invincible fore-runner.

旅行者啊，
你的尾巴朝一旁微微卷起，
如同一位穿着燕尾服的绅士。

不可征服的先驱啊，
所有的生命都在你的肩上。

Tortoise Shout

I thought he was dumb,
I said he was dumb,
Yet I've heard him cry.

First faint scream,
Out of life's unfathomable dawn,
Far off, so far, like a madness, under the horizon's dawning rim,
Far, far off, far scream.

Tortoise in extremis.

Why were we crucified into sex?
Why were we not left rounded off, and finished in ourselves,
As we began,
As he certainly began, so perfectly alone?

A far, was-it-audible scream,
Or did it sound on the plasm direct?

Worse than the cry of the new-born,
A scream,
A yell,
A shout,

乌龟的呼喊

我以为他不会说话，
我说过他是哑巴，
可我听到了他的呼喊。

起先是微弱的尖叫，
来自生命的深奥的黎明，
在遥远的地方，像发狂，在刚刚显现的地平线下，
遥远的地方，遥远的尖叫。

临终之时的乌龟。

我们为何被钉在性的十字架上？
我们为何不能圆满地留下，在自己的身上结束，
如同我们开始，
如同他的开始，完全地孤独？

遥远的、勉强可辨的尖叫，
或许直接响在血浆里？

糟于新生儿的哭喊，
一声尖叫，
一声呼喊，
一声叫嚣，

A paean,

A death-agony,

A birth-cry,

A submission,

All tiny, tiny, far away, reptile under the first dawn.

War-cry, triumph, acute-delight, death-scream reptilian,

Why was the veil torn?

The silken shriek of the soul's torn membrane?

The male soul's membrane

Torn with a shriek half music, half horror.

Crucifixion.

Male tortoise, cleaving behind the hovel-wall of that dense female,

Mounted and tense, spread-eagle, out-reaching out of the shell

In tortoise-nakedness,

Long neck, and long vulnerable limbs extruded, spread-eagle

over her house-roof,

And the deep, secret, all-penetrating tail curved beneath her walls,

Reaching and gripping tense, more reaching anguish in

uttermost tension

Till suddenly, in the spasm of coition, tupping like a jerking

leap, and oh!

Opening its clenched face from his outstretched neck

一支赞歌，

一声咽气时的呻吟，

一声诞生时的哭嚷，

一次降服，

全都微弱难辨，极为遥远，在曙光下忽隐忽现。

战场上的喊叫，胜利，尖锐的高兴，卑鄙的死亡的尖叫，

面纱为何撕破？

灵魂之膜破裂而发出丝一般的尖叫声？

雄性灵魂之膜

随着一半音乐、一半恐惧的尖叫而撕破。

钉在十字架上。

雄的乌龟，在严密的雌性乌龟的陋屋后面穿过，

架好，拉紧，像展翅的鹰，经乌龟的赤裸

从壳体中伸出，

长长的脖颈、长长的脆弱的四肢伸了出来，展翅的鹰在她

　　的屋顶上，

深深的，秘密的，穿透一切的尾巴弯曲在她的墙壁之下，

延伸，握紧，以最大的张力延伸更多的痛苦，

直至突然地、在交配的激动中，痉挛地撞击，并且，噢！

从伸出来的颈上，打开捏紧的脸，

And giving that fragile yell, that scream,

Super-audible,

From his pink, cleft, old-man's mouth,

Giving up the ghost,

Or screaming in Pentecost, receiving the ghost.

His scream, and his moment's subsidence,

The moment of eternal silence,

Yet unreleased, and after the moment, the sudden, startling jerk of

    coition, and at once

The inexpressible faint yell—

And so on, till the last plasm of my body was melted back

To the primeval rudiments of life, and the secret.

So he tups, and screams

Time after time that frail, torn scream

After each jerk, the longish interval,

The tortoise eternity,

Agelong, reptilian persistence,

Heart-throb, slow heart-throb, persistent for the next spasm.

I remember, when I was a boy,

I heard the scream of a frog, which was caught with his foot in the

    mouth of an up-starting snake;

发出微弱的呼喊，发出尖叫，

非常响亮，

从他粉红的、咧开的老人的嘴里，

放走灵魂，

或在圣灵降临节发出尖叫，接待神灵。

他的尖叫，他的瞬间的平息，

永恒的寂静时刻，

然而仍未清除，过了一瞬，突然的交配的震颤，立

   刻又发出

无法表述的微弱的叫声——

等等，直到我身体中最后的血浆往回融化成

生命的原始雏形，融化成秘密。

他就这样交尾，他不时尖叫，

微弱的、被撕碎的尖叫发生在

每次急促的动作之后，稍长的停顿，

乌龟的永恒，

长时期的、爬行动物的坚忍，

狂热的心跳、缓慢的心跳，坚忍地等待下一次突发

   的痉挛。

我记得，当我还是孩子的时候，

我听到了青蛙的尖叫，当它的脚被猛然跳起的蛇抓

   进嘴里；

I remember when I first heard bull-frogs break into sound in the
spring;
I remember hearing a wild goose out of the throat of night
Cry loudly, beyond the lake of waters;
I remember the first time, out of a bush in the darkness, a
nightingale's piercing cries and gurgles startled the depths of
my soul;
I remember the scream of a rabbit as I went through a wood at
midnight;
I remember the heifer in her heat, blorting and blorting through
the hours, persistent and irrepressible;
I remember my first terror hearing the howl of weird, amorous
cats;
I remember the scream of a terrified, injured horse, the sheet-
lightning,
And running away from the sound of a woman in labor, something
like an owl whooing,
And listening inwardly to the first bleat of a lamb,
The first wail of an infant,
And my mother singing to herself,
And the first tenor singing of the passionate throat of a young
collier, who has long since drunk himself to death,
The first elements of foreign speech
On wild dark lips.

我记得我第一次听到牛蛙在春天里突然喧嚷起来；

我记得我听见一只野鹅在湖的那边，

从夜的喉咙中发出高声叫喊；

我记得一只夜莺在黑暗中从灌木丛里撕出尖叫和咯

　　咯声，第一次震惊了我的心灵深处；

我记得兔子的尖叫，当我在子夜穿越树林；

我记得发情的小母牛持续不断地哞哞直叫，压抑不

　　住自己；

我记得当我第一次听到恋爱中的猫发出怪诞的号

　　叫，我是多么恐惧；

我记得受到惊吓和伤害的马儿的尖叫、片状闪电，

我记得我被临产的妇女的叫声吓跑，那声音就像猫

　　头鹰的怪叫，

我记得我暗自听着初次的羊咩、

婴儿的初次号啕、

我妈妈的自我歌唱、

酩酊大醉的年轻矿工醒酒之后放开激情的嗓门发出

　　的第一声高喊，

以及从粗野的黑色嘴唇中

吐出的头几个外国词语。

And more than all these,

And less than all these,

This last,

Strange, faint coition yell

Of the male tortoise at extremity,

Tiny from under the very edge of the farthest far-off horizon of life.

The cross,

The wheel on which our silence first is broken,

Sex, which breaks up our integrity, our single inviolability, our

    deep silence,

Tearing a cry from us.

Sex, which breaks us into voice, sets us calling across the deeps,

    calling, calling for the complement,

Singing, and calling, and singing again, being answered,

    having found.

Torn, to become whole again, after long seeking for what is lost,

The same cry from the tortoise as from Christ, the Osiris-cry

    of abandonment,

That which is whole, torn asunder,

That which is in part, finding its whole again throughout

    the universe.

但极端处境中的雄龟
发出的最后一声
奇异、微弱的相交的叫喊，
从遥远遥远的生命地平线的边缘发出的微弱的叫喊，
强于我记忆中的一切声音，
弱于我记忆中的一切声音。

十字架，
首先打破我们沉默的旋转，
性，击碎了我们的完整、我们单独的神圣
　　　以及我们深深的沉默，
从我们身上撕出一声叫喊。

性，把我们劈成声音，迫使我们透过深处，呼唤，呼
　　　唤，为整体的完善而呼唤，
歌唱、呼唤，再次歌唱，得到了回答，找到了所寻。

撕碎，为了再次变得完整，经过对于失落之物的长久
　　　的找寻，
乌龟身上的叫喊仿佛来自基督的身上，地狱判官的
　　　放任的叫喊，
整体的东西被撕成散片，
分散的部分通过宇宙又找到了整体。

We Are Transmitters

As we live, we are transmitters of life.
And when we fail to transmit life, life fails to flow through us.

That is part of the mystery of sex, it is a flow onwards.
Sexless people transmit nothing.

And if, as we work, we can transmit life into our work,
life, still more life, rushes into us to compensate, to be ready
and we ripple with life through the days.

Even if it is a woman making an apple dumpling, or a man a stool,
if life goes into the pudding, good is the pudding
good is the stool,
content is the woman, with fresh life rippling in her,
content is the man.

Give, and it shall be given unto you
is still the truth about life.
But giving life is not so easy.
It doesn't mean handing it out to some mean fool, or letting the
    living dead eat you up.
It means kindling the life-quality where it was not,
even if it's only in the whiteness of a washed pocket-handkerchief.

我们是生命的传送者

当我们生存，我们是生命的传送者。
当我们不能传送生命，生命就不再流经我们。

这就是性的部分神秘，这是向前的流动。
无性的人们无物传送。

我们工作时，如果我们能把生命传送进工作，
生命就更富有生命，冲入我们身上作为补偿，作好准备，
我们与生命在时光之洋上发出涟漪。

即使是一个女人在做布丁，或一个男人在做板凳，
如果生命进入布丁，布丁就会优美，
凳子就会优美，
这位女人就会满意，清新的生命带着涟漪注入她的身上，
这位男人就会欢畅。

奉献乃是生活的真谛，
应该向你作出奉献。
但奉献生命并非易事。
并不是把生命递给哪位下贱的蠢货，或让活着的死人把
    你吃掉。
而是在无德性的地方燃起生命的品德，
哪怕它只存在于洗净的手绢的洁白之中。

Spray

It is a wonder foam is so beautiful.
A wave bursts in anger on a rock, broken up
in wild white sibilant spray
and falls back, drawing in its breath with rage,
with frustration how beautiful!

浪花

奇怪，海沫如此美丽！
海浪愤怒地冲击岩石，
裂成咝咝发闹的白色的野性浪花，
接着撤退，狂暴地吸气，
这样失败多么美丽！

The Mess of Love

We've made a great mess of love
since we made an ideal of it.

The moment I swear to love a woman, a certain woman, all my life
that moment I begin to hate her.

The moment I even say to a woman: I love you!—
my love dies down considerably.

The moment love is an understood thing between us, we are sure of it,
it's a cold egg, it isn't love any more.

Love is like a flower, it must flower and fade;
if it doesn't fade, it is not a flower,
it's either an artificial rag blossom, or an immortelle, for the cemetery.

The moment the mind interferes with love, or the will fixes on it,
or the personality assumes it as an attribute, or the ego takes possession
    of it,
it is not love any more, it's just a mess.
And we've made a great mess of love, mind-perverted, will-perverted,
    ego-perverted love.

爱情大杂烩

自从我们把爱情想得完美，
我们就已经把爱情弄糟。

我起誓一辈子爱某个女人的时刻，
也就是我开始恨她的时分。

甚至当我对女人说"我爱你！"的时候，
我的爱情就大幅度地消亡。

当爱情被我俩理解，我们已对此确信，
它就成了一只冷蛋，它再也不是爱情。

爱情就像鲜花，必须开放，必须凋谢，
如果不凋谢，那就不是鲜活的爱情，
只是装饰坟墓的人造布花，或蜡菊。

当心灵与爱情发生冲突，或意志选定了爱情，
或人格把它当品质来重现，或自我把它当财物来占有，
它就不再是爱情，只是大杂烩。
我们已经制作了爱情大杂烩，扭曲心灵的、扭曲意
    志的、扭曲自我的爱情。

Fidelity

Fidelity and love are two different things, like a flower and a gem.
And love, like a flower, will fade, will change into something else
or it would not be flowery.

O flowers, they fade because they are moving swiftly; a little
    torrent of life
leaps up to the summit of the stem, gleams, turns over round
    the bend
of the parabola of curved flight,
sinks, and is gone, like a comet curving into the invisible.

O flowers they are all the time travelling
like comets, and they come into our ken
for a day, for two days, and withdraw, slowly vanish again.

And we, we must take them on the wing, and let them go.
Embalmed flowers are not flowers, immortelles are not flowers;
flowers are just a motion, a swift motion, a coloured gesture;
that is their loveliness. And that is love.

But a gem is different. It lasts so much longer than we do
so much much much much longer
that it seems to last forever.

忠贞

忠贞与爱情不是一码事，如同鲜花与宝石。
爱情，就像鲜花，将会凋谢，将会转变成别的东西，
否则就算不上绚丽。

噢，鲜花凋谢，因为它们疾速运动；小小的生命湍流
跃上茎的顶巅，隐约闪现，疯狂旋动
急转弯飞翔时的抛物线，
下倾，离去，像一颗彗星急速拐进幽冥世界。

噢，鲜花始终在运行，
如同彗星，它们进入我们的认知领域，
一天，两天，随后撤回，再次慢悠悠地消亡。

我们，我们必须给它们装上翅膀，放它们离开。
香味弥漫的花不算花，灰毛菊不算花；
花只是一种运动，一种疾速的运动，
一种绚丽多彩的动作姿态；
这就是它们的可爱。这就是爱情。

但宝石迥然不同。它一个劲儿地延续，
存在得比我们更为长久，
似乎要永世长存。

Yet we know it is flowing away

as flowers are, and we are, only slower.

The wonderful slow flowing of the sapphire!

All flows, and every flow is related to every other flow.

Flowers and sapphires and us, diversely streaming.

In the old days, when sapphires were breathed upon and

    brought forth

during the wild orgasms of chaos

time was much slower, when the rocks came forth.

It took aeons to make a sapphire, aeons for it to pass away.

And a flower it takes a summer.

And man and woman are like the earth, that brings forth flowers

in summer, and love, but underneath is rock.

Older than flowers, older than ferns, older than foraminiferae,

older than plasm altogether is the soul of a man underneath.

And when, throughout all the wild orgasms of love

slowly a gem forms, in the ancient, once-more-molten rocks

of two human hearts, two ancient rocks, a man's heart and

    a woman's,

that is the crystal of peace, the slow hard jewel of trust,

the sapphire of fidelity.

The gem of mutual peace emerging from the wild chaos of love.

然而我们知道它不断地消亡，
如同鲜花，如同我们，只是更为缓慢。
蓝宝石的美妙的缓慢的消亡！

一切都在流逝，每一种流逝都与另一种流逝发生联系。
鲜花和宝石，还有我们，互不相同地流逝。
在昔日，当宝石被玷污，被诱惑，
在混乱的疯狂高潮，
当岩石诞生时，时光缓慢得多。
它花了无数的年代造就的宝石，也要花无数的年代让
　　宝石消亡。

一朵花只有一个夏天。

男人和女人就像泥土，生出夏天的鲜花和爱情，
但下方就是岩石。
比鲜花年长，比羊齿植物年长，比有孔虫类年长，
比所有的原形质都要年长——这就是下方的人的灵魂。

在全部的爱情疯狂高潮，
宝石缓慢地形成，在古老的、曾经融合的两颗心脏的
　　岩石中，
两个古老的岩石，男人和女人的两颗心脏，
这是宁静之结晶，是缓慢坚固的信任之珠宝，
是忠贞之蓝宝石。
从爱情疯狂的混乱中，共同宁静之宝石脱颖而出。

What Would You Fight for?

I am not sure I would always fight for my life.
Life might not be worth fighting for.

I am not sure I would always fight for my wife.
A wife isn't always worth fighting for.

Nor my children, nor my country, nor my fellow men.
It all depends whether I found them worth fighting for.

The only thing men invariably fight for
is their money. But I doubt if I'd fight for mine, anyhow,
    not to shed a lot of blood over it.

Yet one thing I do fight for, tooth and nail, all the time.
And that is my bit of inward peace, where I am at one with myself.

And I must say, I am often worsted.

你究竟为何奋斗？

我不确定我是否始终为生活而奋斗，
生活也许并不值得为之拼搏。

我不清楚我是否始终为妻子而奋斗，
一个妻子并不始终值得为她矢志不渝。

同样还有孩子、国家，以及同胞，
这全都取决于我是否发现值得为他们付出。

人们亘古不变为之奋斗的唯一东西——
便是金钱，但是我怀疑我能否为之而战，至少不会战
　　　得头破血流。

然而，有件东西我得始终为之拼命奋斗，
那就是内心的一片宁静，只有在内心我才能成为自己。

我必须说明，我也常吃败仗。

Fire

Fire is dearer to us than love or food,

hot, hurrying, yet it burns if you touch it.

What we ought to do

is not to add our love together, or our goodwill, or any of that,

for we're sure to bring in a lot of lies,

but our fire, our elemental fire

so that it rushes up in a huge blaze like a phallus into

    hollow space

and fecundates the zenith and the nadir

and sends off millions of sparks of new atoms

and singes us, and burns the house down.

火

对于我们，火比爱情或食物更亲近，
炽热、急促，一旦触击就会燃烧。
我们该做的就是
不要把我们的爱情加在一起，或我们的善意，或类
　　似的东西，
因为肯定会带入很多谎言，
但把我们的火，自然力的火加在一起，
好让它腾起巨大的火焰，像阴茎伸进空荡荡的空间，
使天顶和天底受孕，
放射出千百万新原子的火花
烧毁我们，烧毁下方的房屋。

Nemesis

The Nemesis that awaits our civilisation

is social insanity

which in the end is always homicidal.

Sanity means the wholeness of the consciousness.

And our society is only part conscious, like an idiot.

If we do not rapidly open all the doors of consciousness

and freshen the putrid little space in which we are cribbed

the sky-blue walls of our unventilated heaven

will be bright red with blood.

复仇女神

等待我们现代文明的复仇女神
是最终杀人成性的
全社会的疯狂。
公正明达意味着意识的健全。
我们的社会只有部分意识，像一名白痴。

如果我们不急速打开意识的所有大门，
使禁锢我们的腐烂小空间显得清新，
我们通风不良的苍穹的湛蓝墙壁
就会被鲜血染得通红通红。

Self-Protection

When science starts to be interpretive
it is more unscientific even than mysticism.

To make self-preservation and self-protection the first law
      of existence
is about as scientific as making suicide the first law of existence,
and amounts to very much the same thing.

A nightingale singing at the top of his voice
is neither hiding himself nor preserving himself nor propa-
      gating his species;
he is giving himself away in every sense of the word;
and obviously, it is the culminating point of his existence.

A tiger is striped and golden for his own glow.
He would certainly be much more invisible if he were
      grey-green.

And I don't suppose the ichthyosaurus sparkled like the
      humming-bird,
no doubt he was khaki-coloured with muddy protective
      coloration,
so why didn't he survive?

自我保护

当科学开始被用来解释，
它甚至比神秘主义更不科学。

把自我保护变成生存的第一法则，
就如同把自杀变成生存的第一法则一样科学，
两者就是一回事情。

一只夜莺放开嗓子高唱，
既没有隐藏自己、保护自己，也没有繁殖自己的种类；
他是在名符其实地奉献自己；
显而易见，这是他生存的极点。

一只老虎身披金色条纹，光彩耀眼。
他若是灰绿色就不会引人注目。

我知道鱼龙不会像蜂鸟一样闪光，
也不怀疑他有自己的保护色——土色，
但他为何没有生存下来？

As a matter of fact, the only creatures that seem to survive

are those that give themselves away in flash and sparkle

and gay flicker of joyful life;

those that go glittering abroad

with a bit of splendour.

Even mice play quite beautifully at shadows,

and some of them are brilliantly piebald.

I expect the dodo looked like a clod,

a drab and dingy bird.

实际上，想要幸存的生物，
只有在闪光和燃烧中奉献自己，
快乐地扑闪着欢欣的生命；
身披光彩，
闪闪发光地走向外部世界。

甚至连老鼠也美妙地与光影嬉戏，
有一些变得色彩斑驳。

我料想渡渡鸟似泥土一块，[1]
毫无生气的黑暗的鸟。

---

1 渡渡鸟：一种产于毛里求斯的鸟，现已经绝种，常用来比喻落后于时代的人、
糊涂虫等。

Volcanic Venus

What has happened in the world?
the women are like little volcanoes
all more or less in eruption.

It is very unnerving, moving in a world of smouldering volcanoes.
It is rather agitating, sleeping with a little Vesuvius.

And exhausting, penetrating the lava-crater of a tiny Ixtaccihuatl
and never knowing when you'll provoke an earthquake.

火山爆发般的性爱

世界上发生了什么事情?
女人如同一座座火山
或多或少具有喷发的可能。

在有许多火山闷烧的世上，极不平静，令人身心俱疲。
同小小的维苏威睡觉，岂不令人焦虑。[1]

胆战心惊啊，当你进入伊斯塔西华特尔的火山口，[2]
并且从不知道你何时会引起一场地震。

1　维苏威：意大利火山名。
2　伊斯塔西华特尔：墨西哥的火山名，又名"沉睡的女人"。

Conundrums

Tell me a word
that you've often heard,
yet it makes you squint
if you see it in print!

Tell me a thing
that you've often seen,
yet if put in a book
it makes you turn green!

Tell me a thing
that you often do,
which described in a story
shocks you through and through!

Tell me what's wrong
with words or with you
that you don't mind the thing
yet the name is taboo.

谜

告诉我一个词儿，
你经常能够听见，
然而一旦印到纸上，
你就对它斜眼！

告诉我一件事情，
你经常能够目睹，
然而一旦写进书里，
就会使你嫉妒！

告诉我一种行动，
你经常能够从事，
然而一旦在故事中描述，
你就会无比惊悸！

告诉我词儿错在哪里，
或者你自己错在哪里，
你不介意具体行动，
名称却遭到禁忌。

Desire

Ah, in the past, towards rare individuals

I have felt the pull of desire:

Oh come, come nearer, come into touch!

Come physically nearer, be flesh to my flesh—

But say little, oh say little,

and afterwards, leave me alone.

Keep your aloneness, leave me my aloneness.

I used to say this, in the past—but now no more.

It has always been a failure.

They have always insisted on love

and on talking about it

and on the me-and-thee and what we meant to each other.

So now I have no desire any more

Except to be left, in the last resort, alone, quite alone.

愿望

唉，在昔日，对于罕见的美人，
我感觉到一种愿望：
来吧，更近一些；接触在一起！
生理上的接近，肉体靠近肉体——

少说些话，哦，少说些话，
然后，离开我，让我独居。
保持你的孤独，也尊重我的孤独。
我过去常常这么说，但现在我不再多说，
总是归于失败。
她们总是强调爱情，
不停地谈论爱情，
不停地卿卿我我，唠叨着彼此在对方心中的位置。

所以我现在再也没有别的愿望，
只剩下最后一着：让我孤独，完全地孤独！

Intimates

Don't you care for my love? she said bitterly.

I handed her the mirror, and said:
Please address these questions to the proper person!
Please make all requests to headquarters!
In all matters of emotional importance
please approach the supreme authority direct!
So I handed her the minor.

And she would have broken it over my head,
but she caught sight of her own reflection
and that held her spellbound for two seconds
while I fled.

知己

你不关心我的爱情？她痛苦地说。

我把镜子递给她，说：
请向合适的人提这类问题！
请向司令部发出请求！
有关情感重要性方面的事务，
请你直接与最高当局接头！
于是我把镜子递给了她。

她本会把镜子砸碎在我的脑袋，
但她瞥见了自己的镜中形象，
被迷住了几秒时间，
我乘机逃得无影无踪。

True Love at Last

The handsome and self-absorbed young man
looked at the lovely and self-absorbed girl
and thrilled.

The lovely and self-absorbed girl
looked back at the handsome and self-absorbed young man
and thrilled.

And in that thrill he felt:
Her self-absorption is even as strong as mine.
I must see if I can't break through it
And absorb her in me.

And in that thrill she felt:
His self-absorption is even stronger than mine!
What fun, stronger than mine!
I must see if I can't absorb this Samson of self-absorption.

So they simply adored one another
and in the end
they were both nervous wrecks, because
in self-absorption and self-interest they were equally
    matched.

最终实现的真正的爱情

英俊而自私自利的少男
望着美丽而自私自利的少女，
一阵震颤。

自私自利的美丽少女
回望着自私自利的英俊少男，
一阵震颤。

他在一阵震颤中感到：
她的自私自利甚至像我一样强烈。
我必须弄清我能否把它突破，
使她对我发生兴趣。

她在一阵震颤中感到：
他的自私自利甚至比我更强！
多么有趣，比我更强！
我必须弄清我能否吞并这位自私自利的大力士。

于是他俩简单地相互爱慕，
最终，
两人都被刮成痉挛的破船，
因为在自私自利方面他俩不相上下，般配无比。

Fatality

No one, not even God, can put back a leaf on to a tree
once it has fallen off.

And no one, not God nor Christ nor any other,
can put back a human life into connection with the living
    cosmos
once the connection has been broken
and the person has become finally self-centred.

Death alone, through the long process of disintegration,
can melt the detached life back
through the dark Hades at the roots of the tree
into the circulating sap, once more, of the tree of life.

命运

一旦树叶凋落，
甚至连上帝也不能使它返回树身。

一旦人类生活与活生生的宇宙的联系被击破，
人最后变得以自我为中心，
不管什么人，不管是上帝还是基督，
都无法挽回这种联系。

只有死亡通过分解的漫长过程，
能够融化分裂的生活。
经过树根旁边的黑暗的冥河，
再次融进生命之树的流动的汁液。

In a Spanish Tram-Car

She fanned herself with a violet fan
and looked sulky, under the thick straight brows.

The wisp of modern black mantilla
made her half Madonna, half Astarte.

Suddenly her yellow-brown eyes looked with a flare
    into mine.
—We could sin together! —

The spark fell and kindled instantly on my blood,
then died out almost as swiftly.

She can keep her sin
She can sin with some thick-set Spaniard.
Sin doesn't interest me.

在一辆西班牙电车上

她扇着一把紫罗兰色的扇子，
两道眉毛挺得笔直，显得郁郁不乐。

一缕现代的黑色头纱
使她一半像圣母，一半像阿斯达特。[1]

突然她黄褐色的眼睛带着闪光看着我的眼睛。
——我们能够一起犯罪！——

火光落在我的血中，瞬间燃烧，
接着又迅速地消逝而去。

她能够坚持犯罪，
她能够与某个狡黠的西班牙人作恶。
可作恶不会引起我的兴趣。

---

1 阿斯达特：拜伦诗剧《曼弗雷德》中的人物，是主人公曼弗雷德热恋的神秘
的女子。

Trees in the Garden

Ah in the thunder air
how still the trees are!

And the lime tree, lovely and tall, every leaf silent,
hardly looses even a last breath of perfume.

And the ghostly, creamy coloured little tree of leaves,
white, ivory white among the rambling greens,
how evanescent, variegated elder, she hesitates on the green grass
as if, in another moment, she would disappear
with all her grace of foam!

And the larch that is only a column, it goes up too tall to see:
and the balsam-pines that are blue with the grey-blue blueness of
        things from the sea,
and the young copper beech, its leaves red-rosey at the ends,
how still they are together, they stand so still
in the thunder air, all strangers to one another
as the green grass glows upwards, strangers in the silent garden.

花园里的树

啊，在雷声轰鸣的空气中，
树木却泰然自若！

可爱的高大的椴树。叶儿寂然无声，
不再丢失最后的一口芳香。

幽灵一般，奶油色的小树，
乳白色的叶儿点缀在蔓延的绿色之中，
多么轻盈，斑驳的接骨木，她在绿草中踌躇，
仿佛她转瞬间就会消失，
带着她全部布满泡沫的雅致！

只剩圆柱的落叶松，高得看不到顶，
枞树披着摄于碧海的蔚蓝，
年轻的叶色似铜的山毛榉，叶端粉红，
他们多么寂静地站在一起，默默地站在
雷声轰鸣的空气中，彼此陌生，
像长入空中的绿草，寂静之园的生客。

Whales Weep Not!

They say the sea is cold, but the sea contains
the hottest blood of all, and the wildest, the most urgent.

All the whales in the wider deeps, hot are they, as they urge
on and on, and dive beneath the icebergs.
The right whales, the sperm-whales, the hammer-heads, the killers
there they blow, there they blow, hot wild white breath out of the sea!

And they rock, and they rock, through the sensual ageless ages
on the depths of the seven seas,
and through the salt they reel with drunk delight
and in the tropics tremble they with love
and roll with massive, strong desire, like gods.
Then the great bull lies up against his bride
in the blue deep bed of the sea,
as mountain pressing on mountain, in the zest of life:
and out of the inward roaring of the inner red ocean of whale blood
the long tip reaches strong, intense, like the maelstrom-tip, and
        comes to rest
in the clasp and the soft, wild clutch of a she-whale's fathomless body.

And over the bridge of the whale's strong phallus, linking the
        wonder of whales

白鲸不会哭泣

人们说海水寒冷，但海中含有
最热的、最具野性的、最急切的鲜血。

在辽阔的深海中，所有的白鲸血气方刚，
不断奋进，潜泳在流冰之下。
露脊鲸、巨头鲸、双髻鲨、逆戟鲸，
他们全在喘气，全在喘气，从大海冒出狂暴的白色的
        呼吸！

他们摇摇摆摆，穿过耽于声色口腹的永恒的世纪，
在七大海洋的深处，
他们以陶醉的欢乐摇晃着，越过盐沼，
他们满怀爱恋，在热带颤动，
并以巨大、强烈的愿望向前摇晃颠簸，如同诸神。
接着，雄鲸躺上了他的新娘，
在蓝色的大海之床，
像一座高山以其生命的热忱压上了另一座高山；
离开白鲸内部红色血海的沸腾，
长长的顶端达到了强壮和剧烈，像一股巨大的旋流，
然后停留在雌鲸深不可测的体内，休息在柔软而又粗
        暴的紧握之中。

在白鲸强壮的、连接奇迹的阴茎之桥上，

the burning archangels under the sea keep passing, back and forth,

keep passing, archangels of bliss

from him to her, from her to him, great Cherubim

that wait on whales in mid-ocean, suspended in the waves of the

    sea,

great heaven of whales in the waters, old hierarchies.

And enormous mother whales lie dreaming, suckling their whale-

    tender young

and dreaming with strange whale eyes wide open in the waters of

    the beginning and the end.

And bull-whales gather their women and whale-calves in a ring

when danger threatens, on the surface of the ceaseless flood,

and range themselves like great fierce Seraphim facing the threat,

encircling their huddled monsters of love.

And all this happens in the sea, in the salt

where God is also love, but without words:

and Aphrodite is the wife of whales

most happy, happy she!

and Venus among the fishes skips and is a she-dolphin,

she is the gay, delighted porpoise sporting with love and the sea,

she is the female tunny-fish, round and happy among the males

and dense with happy blood, dark rainbow bliss in the sea.

燃烧着的大天使不停地在海水下面来回穿越，
不停地穿越，极乐的大天使
从他越向她，从她越向他，了不起的小天使
等在海洋中部的白鲸上面，悬浮在大海的波浪之中，
水中的巨大的白鲸天国，古老的统治集团。

庞大无比的白鲸母亲神情恍惚地躺着，给娇嫩的幼鲸
　　喂奶，
神情恍惚，但在既是起源又是终极的水中睁圆了奇特的
　　双眼。

一旦危险来临，雄鲸围成一圈，
护卫他们的妇女和鲸仔，在永不平息的水面，
围成一圈，像勇猛的六翼天使，
面临自己的爱人遭受包围的威胁。
这一切发生在海里，发生在上帝也是爱情的盐沼，
但发生得无声无息；
阿佛洛狄忒是白鲸的爱妻，
她最为幸福，最为幸福；

维纳斯在鱼群之中跳跃，她是母海豚，
她是欢乐愉快的海豚，与爱情和大海嬉戏，
她是雌金枪鱼，在雄鱼之中耿直、幸福，
充满着狂喜的血液、海中深沉的五彩缤纷的乐趣。

The Ship of Death

I

Now it is autumn and the falling fruit

and the long journey towards oblivion.

The apples falling like great drops of dew

to bruise themselves an exit from themselves.

And it is time to go, to bid farewell

to one's own self, and find an exit

from the fallen self.

II

Have you built your ship of death, O have you?

O build your ship of death, for you will need it.

The grim frost is at hand, when the apples will fall

thick, almost thundrous, on the hardened earth.

And death is on the air like a smell of ashes!

Ah! can't you smell it?

And in the bruised body, the frightened soul

finds itself shrinking, wincing from the cold

that blows upon it through the orifices.

灵船

时值秋天，掉落的水果；
通向湮灭的漫长的征途。

苹果像大颗的露珠一样掉落，
撞破自己，为自己打开一个出口。

该走了，向自我道一声告别，
从掉落的自我中
寻找一个出口。

你是否造好了自己的灵船？
哦，造一只灵船吧，因为你需要它。

严霜很快就要降临，苹果密集地、
几乎轰隆轰隆地向变硬的大地掉落。

死亡就像骨灰的气味一样散发在空气里！
啊！你难道没有闻到吗？

在撞破的躯体内，惊恐的灵魂
发现自己蜷缩一团，无法抵挡
从洞孔吹入而进的寒气。

III

And can a man his own quietus make

with a bare bodkin?

With daggers, bodkins, bullets, man can make

a bruise or break of exit for his life;

but is that a quietus, O tell me, is it quietus?

Surely not so! for how could murder, even self-murder

ever a quietus make?

IV

O let us talk of quiet that we know,

that we can know, the deep and lovely quiet

of a strong heart at peace!

How can we this, our own quietus, make?

V

Build then the ship of death, for you must take

the longest journey, to oblivion.

And die the death, the long and painful death

that lies between the old self and the new.

三

一个人能否用出鞘的剑
来解除生活的苦难？ [1]

用匕首，用长剑，用子弹，
人们能为自己的生命捅开一个出口；
但是，请告诉我，这是否就是解除苦难？

当然不是！一个凶手，一个自杀凶手
怎能解除人生的苦难？

四

哦，让我们谈谈我们所知道的宁静，
我们能够知道的、深切、可爱的宁静，
它来自安谧时分的强烈的心灵！

我们怎能为自己解除苦难？

五

那么为自己制造一只灵船吧，
因为你必须走完最漫长的旅程，抵达湮灭。

面对死亡吧，这漫长而又痛苦的死亡，
摆脱旧的自我，创造新的自我。

1　此处引自莎士比亚《哈姆雷特》第三幕。

Already our bodies are fallen, bruised, badly bruised,
already our souls are oozing through the exit
of the cruel bruise.

Already the dark and endless ocean of the end
is washing in through the breaches of our wounds,
already the flood is upon us.

Oh build your ship of death, your little ark,
and furnish it with food, with little cakes, and wine
for the dark flight down oblivion.

VI

Piecemeal the body dies, and the timid soul
has her footing washed away, as the dark flood rises.

We are dying, we are dying, we are all of us dying
and nothing will stay the death-flood rising within us
and soon it will rise on the world, on the outside world.

We are dying, we are dying, piecemeal our bodies are dying
and our strength leaves us,
and our soul cowers naked in the dark rain over the flood,
cowering in the last branches of the tree of our life.

我们的躯体早就掉落，撞得百孔千疮，
我们的灵魂正从残忍的撞破之处的洞孔，
向外渗漏。

黑暗、无边无际的死亡之洋
正在涌进我们破裂的缺口，
洪水早已把我们覆盖。

哦，造起你的灵船，造起你的避难方舟，
装上食物，装上蛋糕和甜酒，
为了通往湮灭的黑暗的航行。

六

当黑暗的洪水泛起，躯体一点一点地死去，
胆怯的灵魂也被洗劫了立足之处。

我们正在死亡，正在死亡，我们大家正在死亡，
在我们身上升起的死亡洪水不可阻挡，
它很快就会淹没世界，淹没外部世界。

我们正在死亡，正在死亡，我们的躯体正在
　　一点一点地死亡，
我们的力量离开了我们，
我们的灵魂在洪水之上的黑雨中赤身裸体地哆嗦，
在我们的生命之树的最后的枝桠上寒颤。

VII

We are dying, we are dying, so all we can do
is now to be willing to die, and to build the ship
of death to carry the soul on the longest journey.

A little ship, with oars and food
and little dishes, and all accoutrements
fitting and ready for the departing soul.

Now launch the small ship, now as the body dies
and life departs, launch out, the fragile soul
in the fragile ship of courage, the ark of faith
with its store of food and little cooking pans
and change of clothes,
upon the flood's black waste
upon the waters of the end
upon the sea of death, where still we sail
darkly, for we cannot steer, and have no port.

There is no port, there is nowhere to go,
only the deepening blackness darkening still
blacker upon the soundless, ungurgling flood,
darkness at one with darkness, up and down
and sideways utterly dark, so there is no direction any more

七

我们正在死亡，我们正在死亡，我们现在能做的一切
就是心甘情愿地死亡，制作灵船，
带上灵魂去进行最长的一次航行。

小小的船上，准备了木桨和食物，
还有小小的菜盘，以及为辞别的灵魂
所备好的各种用品。

这就开航，随着躯体的死亡
和生命的离别，开航，
易碎的灵魂呆在易碎的勇猛的小舟上，
贮有食物、小小炒锅
和替换衣服的忠诚的方舟，
在一片荒凉的黑色洪水上，
在毁灭之海上，
在死亡之洋上，我们仍旧
糊涂地航行，因为不能掌舵，也没有港口。

没有港口，没地方可去，
只有加深的黑暗在黑暗中继续加深，
在无声的，不是汩汩作响的，与黑暗连成一体的
黑暗的洪水中，上上下下、前前后后、
十足地黑暗，因此，再也没有了方向。

and the little ship is there; yet she is gone.

She is not seen, for there is nothing to see her by.

She is gone! gone! and yet

somewhere she is there.

Nowhere!

VIII

And everything is gone, the body is gone

completely under, gone, entirely gone.

The upper darkness is heavy as the lower,

between them the little ship

is gone,

she is gone.

It is the end, it is oblivion.

IX

And yet out of eternity a thread

separates itself on the blackness,

a horizontal thread

that fumes a little with pallor upon the dark.

Is it illusion? or does the pallor fume

A little higher?

Ah wait, wait, for there's the dawn,

小舟在那儿；然而灵魂已经走了。

她看不见了，附近没有任何物体能看见她。

她已经走了！走了！然而，

她呆在那儿的一个地方。

不知晓的地方！

八

一切都走了，躯体也走了，

完全地走下去了，彻底地走了。

上方的黑暗像下方一样沉重，

在两者之间，小船

已经走了，

灵魂已经走了。

这是终结，这是湮灭。

九

然而，在黑暗之上，

有一条细线从永恒中分离出来，

一条水平线

带着苍白冒到了黑暗之上。

这是幻象？或是苍白

冒得高了一点？

啊，等吧，等吧，因为黎明来了，

the cruel dawn of coming back to life
out of oblivion.

Wait, wait, the little ship
drifting, beneath the deathly ashy grey
of a flood-dawn.

Wait, wait! even so, a flush of yellow
and strangely, O chilled wan soul, a flush of rose.

A flush of rose, and the whole thing starts again.

X

The flood subsides, and the body, like a worn sea-shell,
emerges strange and lovely.
And the little ship wings home, faltering and lapsing
on the pink flood,
and the frail soul steps out, into the house again
filling the heart with peace.

Swings the heart renewed with peace
even of oblivion.

Oh build your ship of death. Oh build it!
for you will need it.
For the voyage of oblivion awaits you.

残酷的黎明从湮灭中，
返回到了人生。

等吧，等吧，小船在漂泊，
在死灰色的
洪水般黎明的下方。

等吧，等吧！虽然如此，但黄色的、奇特的、
冷却的、苍白的灵魂突然萌发，玫瑰突然萌发。

玫瑰突然萌发，一切事物重新开始。

十

洪水平息了，躯体，就像衰旧的海贝，
奇怪地、可爱地浮现出来。
小船急速回家，
在粉红色的洪水上，摇晃，渐渐消失，
易碎的灵魂跳了出来，又回到她自己的家里，
用宁静填塞心房。

被湮灭之宁静复活了的心房
摇荡起来。

哦，造起你的灵船。哦，造起来吧！
因为你将需要它。
因为通往湮灭的航程等着你。

Shadows

And if tonight my soul may find her peace
in sleep, and sink in good oblivion,
and in the morning wake like a new-opened flower
then I have been dipped again in God, and new-created.
And if, as weeks go round, in the dark of the moon
my spirit darkens and goes out, and soft strange gloom
pervades my movements and my thoughts and words,
then I shall know that I am walking still
with God, we are close together now the moon's in shadow.

And if, as autumn deepens and darkens
I feel the pain of falling leaves, and stems that break in storms
and trouble and dissolution and distress
and then the softness of deep shadows folding,
folding around my soul and spirit, around my lips
so sweet, like a swoon, or more like the drowse of a low, sad song
singing darker than the nightingale, on, on to the solstice
and the silence of short days, the silence of the year, the shadow,
then I shall know that my life is moving still
with the dark earth, and drenched
with the deep oblivion of earth's lapse and renewal.

And if, in the changing phases of man's life,

阴影

如果我的灵魂今夜能够在睡眠中
寻到一片安详，沉入美好的湮灭，
并在清晨像新绽的鲜花一样苏醒，
那么，我就会再受浸礼，被重新创造。
如果我的灵魂随着年岁轮回，在月缺中
变得黯淡，离开躯体，柔和的奇特阴郁
弥漫我的行为、我的思想、我的言语，
那么，我就会知晓，我仍与上帝同行，
我们现在亲密地相处在月亮的阴影。

如果我的心灵随着秋意的浓郁和深沉
感受落叶的痛苦，以及树枝在风暴中的折断，
感受深沉阴影笼罩我灵魂时分的
烦恼、瓦解、悲痛，以及随后的温柔，
感受阴影甜美地笼罩我的嘴唇，
似一阵昏厥，或更像昏睡于一曲低沉忧伤的歌，
比夜莺更幽暗的歌一直唱到冬至，
感受短暂至日的寂静，一年的寂静与阴影，
那么，我将会知晓我的生命，
依然随着黑暗的大地而运动，
浸润着大地颓败和更新的深沉湮灭。

如果我在人生的各个转折时期

I fall in sickness and in misery

my wrists seem broken and my heart seems dead

and strength is gone, and my life

is only the leavings of a life:

and still, among it all, snatches of lovely oblivion, and snatches

of renewal,

odd, wintry flowers upon the withered stem, yet new, strange flowers

such as my life has not brought forth before, new blossoms of me—

then I must know that still

I am in the hands of the unknown God,

he is breaking me down to his own oblivion

to send me forth on a new morning, a new man.

因疾病和穷困而落魄潦倒，
手臂似乎断折，心脏似乎死亡，
气力似乎耗尽，我的生命
似乎只是成了一团残渣；

然而其中却有一股可爱的湮灭，一股零散的
冬天鲜花的复兴，从枯萎的茎干绽放而出，
仿佛我的生命中不曾绽放的崭新的奇特鲜花——

那么，我一定依然知晓，
我仍被未知的上帝所掌控，
他正在他的湮灭中将我毁除，
并且在新的黎明把我送向新的生命。

Phoenix

Are you willing to be sponged out, erased, cancelled,
made nothing?
Are you willing to be made nothing?
dipped into oblivion?

If not, you will never really change.

The phoenix renews her youth
only when she is burnt, burnt alive, burnt down
to hot and flocculent ash.
Then the small stirring of a new small bub in the nest
with strands of down like floating ash
Shows that she is renewing her youth like the eagle,
Immortal bird.

凤凰

你愿意被海绵吸干、抹除、勾销，
不复存在？
你愿意不复存在？
湮没无闻？

如果不愿，你永远不会真正地更替。

凤凰要想恢复青春，
只有燃烧自己，活活地燃烧，
烧成炽热的毛状的灰烬。
然后，巢中有新的小东西微微动弹，
带着缕缕柔毛，像飘浮的灰烬，
显示出她已恢复自己的青春，如同雄鹰，
永生不死的凤凰。

Rebuked

How big and white the night is!
I stumble where the shadows lie
Fooling my feet!——does the night-moth
Mock as it flutters by?

Who is it the owl is hooting?
Is it me the dark firs mean
When they point their slanting fingers
With the white of the moon between?

The moon is high——I am little!
She leans forward her smooth pale face
And smiles at my furtive shadow
Dodging behind in disgrace.

指责

夜晚多么巨大，多么苍白！
我绊倒在阴影躺着
愚弄我的双足的地方！——难道
夜之蛾振翼飞行时要把我欺诳？

猫头鹰正在对谁狂叫？
黑色枞树伸着倾斜的手指，
中间夹着月光的皎洁，
这难道就是我的身体？

月亮高高在上，我却如此渺小！
她向前探着平滑的苍白的脸，
朝我行踪秘密的影子微笑，
它耻辱地躲藏到后面。

We Have Gone Too Far

We have gone too far, oh very much too far,
Only attend to the noiseless multitudes
Of ghosts that throng about our muffled hearts.

Only behold the ghosts, the ghosts of the slain,
Behold them homeless and houseless, without complaint
Of their patient waiting upon us, the throng of the ghosts.

And say, what matters any more, what matters,
Save the cold ghosts that homeless flock about
Our serried hearts, drifting without a place?

What matters any more, but only love?
There's only love that matters any more.
There's only love, the rest is all outspent.

Let us receive our ghosts and give them place,
Open the ranks, and let them in our hearts,
And lay them deep in love, lay them to sleep.

The foe can take our goods, our homes and land,
Also the lives that still he may require,
But leave us still to love, still leave us love.

我们已走得太远

我们已走得太远，哦，实在太远，
只请你注意一下无声的众多幽灵
挤压在我们困扰之心的旁边。

只请你看看这些幽灵，这些被杀者的幽灵，
看看他们无家可归，也不诉怨
他们耐心的期待，这些众多的幽灵。

除去这些寒冷的无家可归的幽灵，
没有目标地漂泊，围聚于我们拥挤的心，
再还有什么重要的事情？

还有什么要紧的事，除了爱情？
唯有爱情紧要，唯有爱情。
其余的东西已经衰亡殆尽。

让我们接待我们的幽灵，给他们空间，
撤除卫兵，让他们进入我们的心，
深深地躺在爱情之中，沉入梦境。

敌人能占领我们的房产土地，
也能夺走他仍然所需的生命，
但爱情无法夺走，爱情属于我们。

Leave us to take our ghosts into our hearts,

To lap them round with love, and lay them by

To sleep at last in immemorial love.

We let the weapons slip from out our hands,

We loose our grip, and we unstrain our eyes,

We let our souls be pure and vulnerable.

We cover the houseless dead, so they sleep in peace,

We yield the enemy his last demands,

So he too may be healed, be soothed to peace.

For now the hosts of homeless ghosts do throng

To many about us, so we wander about

Blind with the gossamer of prevalent death.

But let us free our eyes, and look beyond

This serried ecstasy of prevalent death,

And pass beyond, with the foe and the homeless ghosts.

Let us rise up, and go from out this grey

Last twilight of the Gods, to find again

The lost Hesperides where love is pure.

留下我们把幽灵带入心中，
用爱情把他们包裹，安置他们
最终睡进极古的爱情。

我们让武器滑出我们的双手，
我们放松握力，减弱视力，
让我们的灵魂纯洁、敏感。

我们覆盖无家可归的死者，让其宁静入睡，
我们向敌人让步，满足他们的需求，
好让他恢复原状，安宁平静。

现在，极多无家可归的幽灵挤满在
我们的身边，因此我们懵然无知地徘徊，
披着普遍盛行的死亡的薄纱。

但是，让我们双眼澄清，向前观望，
超越普遍死亡的拥挤的恍惚，
超越过去，以及敌人和无家可归的幽灵。

让我们起身，走出神明最后的
灰色的暮光，再次寻回失落的
赫斯珀里得斯，那里爱情纯洁无瑕。[1]

1　赫斯珀里得斯：希腊神话中夜神赫斯珀洛斯的四个女儿，她们负责看守盖亚
作为结婚礼物送给赫拉的金苹果树。

For we have gone too far, oh much too far

Towards the darkness and the shadow of death;

Let us turn back, lest we should all be lost.

Let us go back now, though we give up all

The treasure and the vaunt we ever had,

Let us go back, the only way is love.

因为我们走得太远，哦，实在太远，
朝着黑暗和死亡的阴影；
让我们回头，否则就会失落。

让我们返回吧，尽管我们放弃
我们曾有的全部财富和自负，
让我们返回吧，爱情是唯一的出路。

Rainbow

One thing that is bow-legged

and can't put its feet together

is the rainbow.

Even if the Lord God shouted

—Attention!—

it couldn't put its feet together.

Yet it's got two feet

As you know,

and two pots of gold

we are told.

What I see

when I look at the rainbow

is one foot in the lap of a woman

and one in the loins of a man.

The feet of the arch

that the Lord God rested the worlds on.

And wide, wide apart,

with nothing but desire between them.

虹桥

有个物体是弓形腿，
没法将双脚摆到一起。
这就是虹。

即使上帝大人高喊：
"立正！"
它无法将双脚摆到一起。

然而它有两只脚，
如你所知，
还有两只金瓶，
如人们所说。

当我仰望长虹，
我所看见的是
一只脚在女人的怀里，
一只脚在男人的腰际。

穹窿之脚，
上帝靠它们支撑世界。

广阔地叉开，
两者之间只有欲望。

The two feet of the rainbow

want to put themselves together.

But they can't, or there'd be the vicious circle.

So they leap up like a fountain.

He leaps up, she leaps up,

like rockets!

and they curve over.

From the heart a red ray.

from the brow a gold,

from the hips a violet

leaps.

Dark blue the whole desire leaps

brindled with rays

all of the colours

that leap

and lean over

in the arch

of the rainbow.

They will always do it.

The Lord God said so.

彩虹的两只脚
想并拢到一起。
但是不能，否则就成了畸形的环。

于是它们一跃而起，如同喷泉。
他一跃而起，她一跃而起，
如同两枚火箭！
它们在上方弯成弧形。

从心中射出红光，
从眉头放出金黄，
从臀部跳出
紫罗兰。

全部深蓝色的欲望跳跃着，
被光线弄得绚丽斑驳，
所有的色彩
跳跃

并且依赖
彩虹的
穹窿。

它们将永远如此。
上帝大人这样说过。

If there are pots of gold

they are pails

of the honey of experience

hanging from the shoulders of the rainbow.

But the one thing that is bow-legged

and can't put its feet together

is the rainbow.

Because one foot is the heart of a man

and the other is the heart of a woman.

And these two, as you know,

never meet.

Save they leap

high—

Oh hearts, leap high!

——they touch in mid-heaven like an acrobat

and make a rainbow.

如果有金瓶，
那就是
经验之蜜的容器
从虹的肩膀悬挂下来。

但是那个物体是弓形腿，
没法将双脚摆到一起，
那就是虹。

因为一只脚是男人的心，
另一只脚是女人的心。
这两只脚，如你所知，
永远不会并到一起。

除非它们
高高飞跃——
啊，心啊，高高飞跃吧！
——在半天相撞，如同杂技演员，
并且形成一座虹桥。

Love as an Escape

It is time men took their thoughts off women

And love and sex and all that.

Because they only try to make women and love and sex

An escape from their horror of imprisonment in our civilization.

And since women are inside the prison just as much as men,

The men in the end only hate them because the escape was no escape.

The thing for men to do is to start to pull down money

Pull it down, and prepare for a new fresh house of life.

Then they'd be able to love. Despair can't love, it can only violate.

作为解脱的爱情

现在，男人应该把自己的意念
从女人和性爱中转移出来。
因为他们只是试图把女人和性爱作为一种解脱，
驱除在现代文明中对禁锢的恐惧。

由于女人也禁锢其中，正如男人，
男人最终只会憎恨她们，因为这种解脱根本不是解脱。

男人该做的事情就是打倒金钱，
建造起清新的生命之屋。
然后他们才能恋爱。失望不能导致爱情，只会对她亵渎。

Deeper Than Love

There is love, and it is a deep thing
but there are deeper things than love.

First and last, man is alone.
He is born alone, and alone he dies
and alone he is while he lives, in his deepest self.

Love, like the flowers, is life, growing.
But underneath are the deep rocks, the living rock that lives
     alone
and deeper still the unknown fire, unknown and heavy, heavy
and alone.

Love is a thing of twoness.
But underneath any twoness, man is alone.

And underneath the great turbulent emotions of love, the
     violent herbage,
lies the living rock of a single creature's pride,
the dark, naif pride.
And deeper even than the bedrock of pride
lies the ponderous fire of naked life

比爱情更深沉

有了爱情，爱情很深沉，
但有比爱情更深沉的事物。

最初和最终，人总是孑然一身。
他孤零零地诞生，他孤零零地逝世。
他在深层的自我中，孤零零地生存。

爱情，就像鲜花，是生长着的生命。
但是在根基之下，是深深的岩石，这活生生的岩石孤
     独地生存着，
比无名的火焰更为深沉，无名、沉重，
沉重、孤独。

爱情具有双性。
但在双性的下面，人是孤单的。

在爱情狂热的情感——凶暴的草茎之下，
躺着孤单物体的活生生的傲慢岩石。
黑暗的、天真的傲慢。
甚至比傲慢之岩床更深沉，
躺着裸体生命的沉重的火焰，

with its strange primordial consciousness of justice
and its primordial consciousness of connection.
connection with still deeper, still more terrible life-fire
and the old, old final life-truth.

Love is of twoness, and is lovely
like the living life on the earth.
but below all roots of love lies the bedrock of naked pride,
    subterranean,

and deeper than the bedrock of pride is the primordial fire
    of the middle
which rests in connection with the further forever
    unknowable fire of all things
and which rocks with a sense of connection, religion
and trembles with a sense of truth, primordial consciousness
and is silent with a sense of justice, the fiery primordial
    imperative.

All this is deeper than love
deeper than love.

伴着奇特的原生的正义意识
和原生的连接意识，
连接更加深沉的、更加可怕的生命之焰
和古老的、最终的生命真谛。

爱情具有双性，并且
像地球上的生命一样可爱，
但在爱情的全部根基下，躺着隐藏的赤体傲慢之岩，

比傲慢之岩更深的是中央的原生火焰，
它寂然连接一切物体的永远不可得知的火焰，
它被连接感和宗教观所惊醒，
它被真实感和原生的意识所震颤，
它因正义感、强烈的原生的诫命而沉寂。

这些都比爱情更深沉，
比爱情更深沉。

D. H. Lawrence

Yet one thing I do fight for, tooth and nail, all the time.
And that is my bit of inward peace, where I am at one with myself.

然而，有件东西我得始终为之拼命奋斗，
那就是内心的一片宁静，只有在内心我才能成为自己。

图书在版编目 (CIP) 数据

劳伦斯诗选 = Selected Poems of D. H. Lawrence：英汉对照 /（英）劳伦斯（D. H. Lawrence）著；吴笛译 . -- 北京：外语教学与研究出版社，2018.11
（英诗经典名家名译）
ISBN 978-7-5213-0493-0

Ⅰ . ①劳… Ⅱ . ①劳… ②吴… Ⅲ . ①英语－汉语－对照读物②诗集－英国－现代 Ⅳ . ①H319.4：I

中国版本图书馆 CIP 数据核字 (2018) 第 252670 号

出 版 人　徐建忠
项目策划　吴　浩
责任编辑　易　璐
责任校对　赵雅茹
封面设计　范晔文
版式设计　郭　莹　范晔文
出版发行　外语教学与研究出版社
社　　址　北京市西三环北路 19 号（100089）
网　　址　http://www.fltrp.com
印　　刷　北京铭传印刷有限公司
开　　本　889×1194　1/32
印　　张　8.5
版　　次　2019 年 1 月第 1 版 2019 年 1 月第 1 次印刷
书　　号　ISBN 978-7-5213-0493-0
定　　价　25.00 元

购书咨询：（010）88819926　电子邮箱：club@fltrp.com
外研书店：https://waiyants.tmall.com
凡印刷、装订质量问题，请联系我社印制部
联系电话：（010）61207896　电子邮箱：zhijian@fltrp.com
凡侵权、盗版书籍线索，请联系我社法律事务部
举报电话：（010）88817519　电子邮箱：banquan@fltrp.com
物料号：304930001

记载人类文明
沟通世界文化
www.fltrp.com